1,000,000 Books

are available to read at

Forgotten Books

www.ForgottenBooks.com

Read online
Download PDF
Purchase in print

ISBN 978-1-331-08397-9
PIBN 10142725

1 MONTH OF FREE READING

at

www.ForgottenBooks.com

By purchasing this book you are eligible for one month membership to ForgottenBooks.com, giving you unlimited access to our entire collection of over 1,000,000 titles via our web site and mobile apps.

To claim your free month visit:

www.forgottenbooks.com/free142725

* Offer is valid for 45 days from date of purchase. Terms and conditions apply.

English
Français
Deutsche
Italiano
Español
Português

www.forgottenbooks.com

Mythology Photography **Fiction** Fishing Christianity **Art** Cooking Essays Buddhism Freemasonry Medicine **Biology** Music **Ancient Egypt** Evolution Carpentry Physics Dance Geology **Mathematics** Fitness Shakespeare **Folklore** Yoga Marketing **Confidence** Immortality Biographies Poetry **Psychology** Witchcraft Electronics Chemistry History **Law** Accounting **Philosophy** Anthropology Alchemy Drama Quantum Mechanics Atheism Sexual Health **Ancient History Entrepreneurship** Languages Sport Paleontology Needlework Islam **Metaphysics** Investment Archaeology Parenting Statistics Criminology **Motivational**

HERMAPHRO-DEITY:

The Mystery of Divine Genius.

BY

ELIZA BARTON LYMAN,

AUTHOR OF

"THE COMING WOMAN," "FAMILIAR TALKS ON UNFAMILIAR TOPICS," ETC.

"This is the Mystery that to this day is hidden and kept secret."
Divine Pymander.

"Even the mystery which hath been hid from ages and from generations, but now is made manifest to his saints; to whom God would make known what is the riches of the glory of this mystery among the Gentiles; Which is Christ in You." *Col. i. 26-27.*

Saginaw, Michigan:
SAGINAW PRINTING AND PUBLISHING COMPANY.
1900

84259

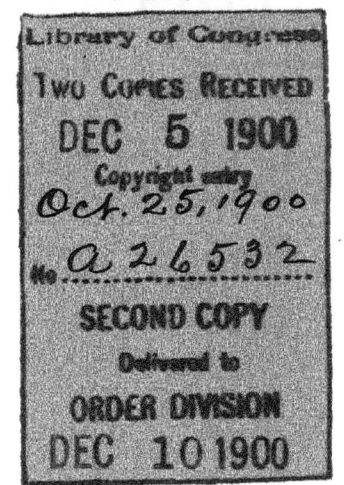

Entered according to Act of Congress, in the year 1900, by
ELIZA BARTON LYMAN,
In the Office of the Librarian of Congress,
at Washington, D. C.

PREFACE.

Hermaphro-Deity is not the result of a desire to present something strange and startling to attract the attention of a public always on the alert for something new and outre, but the outgrowth of a constantly deepening conviction of an approaching crisis in the spiritual experience of the race. No claim is made for the discovery of anything new in either religion, philosophy, or science, but to have simply come into recognition of certain divinely established laws as old as the planet and the race.

The object of this short treatise is to simplify those truths heretofore clothed in deepest mystery. There are a few works upon the subject, but the majority of them are so obscure as to be of little or no service to the general reader; whereas, the truths contained in them should be the property of every individual capable of understanding them.

Whatever view the reader may take of the various philosophies herein laid down, however he may differ with regard to the practical application of the truths advanced; he certainly will be compelled to admit that there is something radically wrong in the arrangement of human affairs, that appears to baffle the best effort toward adjustment and reformation.

Preface.

We feel assured that in this simple work there will be found the law of healing promised the race from remote ages. It was the occult teaching of Jesus, and of all adepts in past ages.

If asked for proofs of many of the statements made, we must needs remain silent—as was Christ before Pilate. We can no more explain how or where we obtained the knowledge of the truths advanced than could Galileo demonstrate to his religious persecutors how or where he obtained the knowledge that the earth was a globe and revolved around its center, the sun. What seemed at that period to be the vagaries of a diseased brain, are today the demonstrated facts of science, accepted by all the world. May it not be possible that in a few generations the new and strange teachings advanced in this brief work will become a demonstrated science, applicable to the deepest needs of human life?

E. B. L.

The Mystery of Divine Genius.

"THE TRUTH IS, A GREAT <u>MIND</u> MUST BE ANDROGYNOUS."

—COLERIDGE.

NOTE.

The quotations from the New Testament are all taken from the Emphatic Diaglott, a version from the original Greek text, by Wilson, giving in some portions quite a different rendition from the old, and more satisfactory.

HERMAPHRO-DEITY:

The Mystery of Divine Genius.

CHAPTER I.

"Girls, come here, please. Sit down; I wish to talk with you on an important matter."

This call came from my brother John's room as we were passing his door on our way out to the porch. We girls, Annie, Angela and myself, walked in submissively, and seated ourselves, as commanded.

John wheeled his chair around facing us, and said, "Girls, I am tired of this sort of life. I believe there is something beyond the mere raising of cabbage and potatoes. Not but what they are good in their proper place; but I have an idea that there are just now subjects and speculations attracting the attention of the thinking world worth investigating, and on quite a different plane of thought. The fact is we get just as hungry for ideas as we do for our daily bread. I have received a letter this morning from an old friend of mine living in Southern California, in a place called Benares, up in the mountains, where a peculiar Order of mystics have established a colony and a school where, he says, if he remembers rightly, are taught those philosophies toward which I have always had a leaning. What he tells me of the fraternity, and some of the tenets held by them, makes me anxious to investigate the matter. This friend of mine," continued John, "has united with the brotherhood. He has been with them some four years, and he thinks I would find in their teachings and practices in life just what I have been looking for all these years. It is not a community of men alone; there are as many women as men. August and Elsie can take care of this place for two or three months without trouble, so what do you girls say to our going and visiting those people."

"Do you really mean that you wish us all to go?" asked Annie in astonishment.

"Certainly. It will take all three of you girls to make one good, all-round woman," answered John, soberly looking down his nose.

We looked at each other in amazement, more than in anger, at the audacity of the speech;

it was our policy never to take notice of any of John's sly slurs on our incapacity and weakness, but to bide our opportunity for retaliation, which never failed to come.

Now there was one peculiarity about John; whenever he made a statement or laid a plan we never thought of disputing or opposing him. So, saying that "we would consider the matter," we retired, and upon due consultation with Angela, who was our oracle, we accept the invitation, for the prospects of a trip to California with such an escort as John caused us to swallow our offence for the time and consent to his arrangements.

So the matter was settled with this understanding, that we should take only hand baggage. "For," said John, "after we leave the Northern Pacific Railroad we have quite a little journey before we reach Benares. After we get up there you girls will have little opportunity to display fine clothing, even if you felt so inclined."

I must give the reader a slight sketch of the leading characteristics of the members of this proposed party, myself excepted; because we are not only to be thrown together in the most intimate relations, but to pass through experiences designed in some cases to change the tenor of the whole life of the individual, and I expect my readers to be as deeply interested in this experience as I have been.

We are orphans, John and myself. He has been my sole guardian for some years, and I had grown to think there was not another human being so perfect as he. At the close of my school life he had left a large city and lucrative position, settling on a farm just outside the corporations of a small town, where, under the management of an efficient German and his wife, with myself installed as housekeeper, there had been established not only a delightful home, but a thoroughly successful and paying institution. We were in the habit of taking a few boarders each summer. I heard John say to a neighbor, "These outsiders coming in will keep Elizabeth"—that is myself—"from being lonely." I had become very proud of my position as mistress of the establishment and fond of the country life.

Annie had been a schoolmate of mine, a close companion. We had closed our school term together, I to go to my brother's home, and she to enter upon an active literary life. She had occupied many responsible positions on the leading periodicals of the day, and was now art correspondent of the finest monthly in the country.

She had spent two years abroad, had written one very successful drama, but what made her of the greatest attraction to me was the fact that she could tell in the most graphic manner anything she knew, and describe what she had seen in a way to make you see it too. She was a source of unspeakable delight to me, who had seen so little of the world. She had become as one of our family, coming each season as soon as the warm weather commenced, staying until autumn.

Angela had spent three seasons with us, and I had grown very fond of her also. She was a quiet, studious woman of thirty years, or thereabout. She was, as a rule, rather silent, but when she did speak she always said something. She was one whom you felt rather than saw. There was about her a power that seemed to penetrate your whole being, your mental, physical and spiritual natures—that is, if one had any such. You somehow felt that she knew everything concerning you. You always wanted to call her mother, and if you had any vexations or troubles you wanted to go to her and tell her all about them, and lay your head on her shoulder and have a good cry. You were always reaching out, if near her, to get hold of her hand. She spent the greater share of her time in the study of curious books with the most unpronounceable names, the contents of which appeared to me, from a casual glance, to be more vague and unattainable than the names even; but that was because I did not comprehend them, Angela had told me. She had traveled much in foreign lands and lived some years in India, which had a tendency to give her a desire for such style of literature.

So much for the two women. It will not be so easy a matter for me to delineate John's character. In the first place it is impossible for a woman to analyze the character of a man correctly, not being of that genus—but the principle reason why I cannot describe John is that I do not understand him. He is a puzzle to me. I love him better than any other being on earth, without being able to understand him. But all women, both old and young, trust him —yes, and love him, too. They tell him all their secrets and troubles and go away from their interviews with him strengthened and comforted apparently. And the men—why, there is a stream of them going to and fro from his "Den," as he calls his office, constantly, much to my disapproval. I have declared all the time that John was working himself to death for Tom, Dick and Harry, and I could see no good in it;

such a loss of time, and I had discovered that it all brought him no money. But, to tell the truth, the man actually did not fail, from the life he led, but instead, to my astonishment, he grew handsomer and more grand looking every year; especially since his hair had commenced falling away, exposing that dome of his head where the phrenologists locate what they claim as intuition, veneration and benevolence. To us girls he is the dearest, most gentle and patient companion, when we need him in that capacity; and when we need the stronger side of his nature he is always ready and willing to use his strong hands, arms and head to help us out of any dilemmas in which we may find ourselves.

One thing that annoys me greatly with him is, that he never has a word of censure or blame for anyone. He always has an excuse for everybody's shortcomings. Always has some good reason why things were thus and so. That always exasperates me. I believe that the people should be brought up standing for their delinquencies; most wrongdoers need a good overhauling to make them straighten up and behave themselves, and that is the reason why, I suppose, that the riff-raff never come to me any more for consolation and assistance, but, instead, all pile on John and Angela for council and aid.

I have often wondered why John has never married, for all the girls dote on him, but he is equally lovely to them all and seems just as fond of the old as he is of the young women. In short, John is a curious being; he is altogether lovely, but queer.

"These are the last days in March and I would like to be in Benares by the first day of April, that will be on Wednesday of next week. In fact, I have written to my friend that I shall be there," John said at the breakfast table the next morning. "There is to be an especially fine course of lessons given at the school, commencing on the second of April," John continued, "and Bessie," turning to me, "I wish you would put me up a few traps, just as few as possible, and let us be off."

"That rascal is just taking us along to mend his socks and put his studs into his clean shirts," said Annie, maliciously, that night as we were preparing for bed. "But after all," she added, half to herself, "he is so very clever, and good to everybody, that one is more than willing to do just what he wants them to, the dear old darling!"

As Angela had traveled throughout India with only hand baggage, Annie and I took lessons from her and we soon were equipped for our journey, but minus "fixin's," as John calls them, and in due time were on our way, speeding toward the setting sun—toward that quarter of the globe that always had such an attraction for me.

THE HOME OF THE MAHATMAS.

Benares, Cal., April 1st.

John's friend, Frederick, met us at the junction of the Northern Pacific Railroad and a branch road leading to the Home of the brotherhood. Although the distance is only a few miles, the ascent is so great that it requires, usually, nearly an hour to reach the "city," as brother Frederick laughingly called the settlement, so that it was ten o'clock before we were inside the Home.

It was too dark for us to form much of an idea of the place. I observed a grove of lofty trees to the right of the town, and behind it there loomed up a great mountain—at least it appeared like one in the darkness. Absolute silence reigned over all—there wasn't even a puff from the old engine that had labored so hard to get us up the hill. At the entrance of the Home building there was an electric light, which gave a very impressive appearance to the structure. As we entered the great hall one of the Sisters, who had awaited our arrival, came forward smilingly, extending her hands, and bade us welcome to Benares.

Brother Frederick took charge of John, conducting him to his apartments, while the Sister leading the way up the stairs ushered us into a large, airy chamber, with all the appointments for three occupants.

I was not so tired but that I began a critical survey of things in general. In the arrangement of the room, everywhere, there was an evidence of woman's artistic eye and hand. The furnishings were of excellent quality, selected with a view to use as well as beauty, and all was immaculately clean. The floor attracted my attention most. It was hardwood, highly polished, of a rich color. The room was lighted with electricity. The air of the whole apartment was soothing in the extreme.

Just here the Sister who had escorted us to our room came in with a tray of refreshments, and informed us that our breakfast would be served in our room in the morning, as we would no doubt feel too much fatigued to rise and breakfast with the family as early as they were in the habit of doing. "We are early risers up here," she said smilingly, "and after a time you will enjoy the morning breezes from the mountains as much as we do." Bidding us good-night she left us to ourselves.

We soon dispatched our lunch and made ourselves ready for bed, as the delightful coolness and fragrance of the air made one inclined to sleep, even had we not been so fatigued from our journey.

"There is something awfully shivery about this whole place," said Annie, "I can almost imagine that I have been suddenly transported to Jupiter or Mars—or some outlandish world —things feel strange and unreal somehow."

"That is all in yourself, my dear, to me it is heavenly," said Angela, taking in a deep breath.

I was too tired to make any comments and in a short time we were all safely stowed away in our delightful beds, and, owing to the fatigue and excitement of the past week, were soon sleeping soundly. A sleep from which I did not awaken until a rap at the door aroused me, and opening my eyes I beheld a perfect flood of sunshine filling the room, and Angela sitting at the open window all dressed and evidently studying the situation outside. Upon opening the door we found our attendant of the previous evening, who informed us that our breakfast would be ready in a few minutes.

"I feel as though I had just been exhumed from the Pyramids of Egypt," yawned Annie, shaking herself and stretching. "I had curious dreams about this place last night," she continued, as she completed her toilet. "I think it is owned and run by a set of fairies, as we see neither men, women or children about the premises."

"I have an evidence of a very different character," said Angela, smiling. "I have been up at the window for more than two hours and have seen at least fifty stalwart men, coming in from the hay fields I concluded, as they all had rakes over their shoulders, broad brimmed hats on their heads and shoes on their feet. True they did not make any noise, but they wore trousers and had no wings."

Our breakfast came at this point and presented a very decidedly human and familiar appearance. It consisted of a plentiful supply of deliciously browned toast, butter, eggs, cream, milk, and a heaping dish of the finest, most luscious strawberries I had ever seen.

Our sweet-voiced attendant informed us, as she was leaving the room after arranging our table, that she would be up about fifteen minutes before nine o'clock to conduct us to the chapel. This being the opening lesson, we would all be expected to be in our places on time. As Father Hyacinth is the teacher for this month no one can afford to lose one word. With that she closed the door and we were 'ft to ourselves to enjoy our most delicious meal.

"How is this breakfast, Annie, has it the taste of the Pyramids and odor of Cheops?" Angela ventured, after watching for a time the greedy manner in which Annie stowed away the food.

"Oh, this is all right! and earthly enough. But I do wonder what they have done with John. If ever a man would be of any use or comfort, it would be in a place like this, where one expects every instant to see a ghost glide in from some hole or corner and to be caught up and spirited away—the Lord only knows where."

After this speech she replenished her dish with strawberries and fell to eating with a gusto most astonishing in one so overcome with fear.

Angela smilingly said, "Do not allow yourself to be terrified, my dear, because whatever the power might be that spirited you away, it would return you as soon as it had had one encounter with you."

Here the door opened and John stalked in looking like a Greek god.

"This is interesting! Do you expect to continne this line of business up here?" he said, affecting great disgust. "It is almost nine o'clock. I have been up for three hours looking over the place; I have been up the mountain a mile, at least, and back, while you girls have been snoozing in bed. This must be the last of these city airs. The men of this community have stacked over fifty tons of hay this morning, while the women have worked over and packed two hundred pounds of butter, taken care of the milk of one hundred and fifty cows, and baked a hundred loaves of bread, besides many delicacies that I cannot mention. They have also made twenty-five large cheeses. And such men and women! but you will see them presently."

The Sister who had brought us our breakfast came in now to conduct us down to the chapel. We all followed our guide down the broad stairway, through the long, wide hall and into the chapel at the rear.

We were seated so that we had a view of the entire room and the audience assembled; there were about three hundred and fifty persons in all, men, women and children, about equally divided as to sex, and seated separately.

At the end of the chapel was a pipe organ, in front of which was a platform, speaker's desk and chair. At our right hung a life-sized painting of Christ and the three Marys; at the left was a fine copy of Murillo's Immaculate Conception. On the easel at the side of the platform was an ideal head of a most beautiful woman, over which, in large letters, were the words, "The Mother." A Sister was seated at the organ, and as she passed her fingers slowly over the keys, the rich, tremulous tones of the instrument quivered through the silent air, producing a feeling of devotion.

I observed that the members of the household all sat motionless with bowed heads. I held my breath and listened. Presently the tones of the organ changed and all broke forth in low subdued tones singing the forty-eighth Psalm: "Great is the Lord, and greatly to be praised in the city of our God, in the mountain of His holiness." The voices taking the different parts all blended in one harmonious wave of melody. I had never cared for hymn singing, but the chanting of the psalm here was inexpressibly solemn and sweet to me.

I had not been much of a church-goer or had any especial religious bias—I was in no sense religiously inclined—but there was something in the air of this room, the music, the people about me, that stirred deep in my nature a feeling that I had never experienced before. Had I been alone with Angela I should have laid my head on her breast and cried a little, but as it was I crept close to John and slipped my hand into his strong, warm one and felt reassured.

As the music and singing ceased, I began studying the people about me.

The first thing that attracted my attention was their dress. The men wore over their ordinary suits a white linen garment made after the fashion of the surplices worn by the Catholic clergy.

Their faces were clean shaven and the hair of the head shingled closely. The back of the head was covered with a black silk cap like those worn by Cardinals.

There was a singular fascination about the group, not only on account of their strange costume, but because of a peculiar expression about the mouth and eyes. This unusual appearance I understood later, as I came to know more of their habit of thought and life.

I turned from the men and began studying the women. Here, as in the case of the men, their costume attracted my notice. It was uniform in color, fabric and style of making. The material was of some soft, light-gray fabric, of wool I should say, that fell in graceful folds from top to bottom, after the fashion of the ancient Greek female costume. There was the long open sleeve ornamented with the Greek pattern in braiding. The costume of the children corresponding. Taking it all together, I had never imagined anything so perfectly artistic and beautiful.

The hair also was uniformly dressed. It was combed back from the forehead and twisted up in a loose knot on the top of the head. In some cases it was as white as snow, in others golden, brown, or black, according to age or temperament.

There was also an unusual expression on the faces of these women, and a kind of peachy tint to the skin that would indicate health and an acquaintance with outdoor life.

At this moment my attention was arrested by the opening of a door at the end of the chapel and the entrance of a man—Father Hyacinth, John informed me—who walked across the room, stepped upon the platform and seated himself, without raising his eyes. I could not take my eyes from him, so remarkable was he in appearance and bearing.

I had never seen but one man whom he resembled, that was Phillips Brooks, during the last years of his ministry, when he had grown so ripe and rich in spiritual grace. This man possessed the same massiveness and silent power and was about the age of Brooks at the time of his death.

He was habited the same as the other male members, and there appeared to be a sort of glory enveloping him that gave one the feeling that to merely touch the hem of his garments would give them new life. When he spoke the charm was complete. His voice was low-keyed, mellow and sympathetic as he unfolded his subject.

"Thought in the Mind hath made us. What we are
    By thought was wrought and built. If a man's mind
Hath evil thoughts, pain comes on him as comes
    The wheel the ox behind.

"All that we are is what we thought and willed;
    Our thoughts shape us and frame. If one endure
In purity of thought, joy follows him
    As his own shadow—sure."

—Edwin Arnold.

"Each individual attracts to himself from others that which he metes out to others. This law of individual compensation is regulated by individual thought, and in such a manner that absolute justice is the portion of each."

—Fragments of the Philosophy.

"He who has succeeded in bringing his individual Mind in exact harmony with the Universal Mind, has succeeded in reuniting the inner sphere with the outer one, from which he has only become separated by mistaking illusions for truths."

—Paracelsus.

FIRST LESSON.

THE DIVINE MIND IN MAN.

I have to make this morning some very important statements as a foundation upon which to base the theories advanced in the forthcoming lessons. Not only should they form the foundation, but they should be a guide with which to square all religions, philosophies, sciences or theories that may present themselves to the student during life. I shall endeavor to employ only such terms as we are most familiar with. It requires but few words to clothe these stupendous truths, which should stand out naked, in their colossal proportions, before the mind of the student, a study full of veneration, as the Alps to the Swiss peasant is a source of worship and strength.

This then is our chief corner-stone:

GOD IS THE ONLY LIFE;
SPIRIT IS THE ONLY SUBSTANCE;
MIND IS THE ONLY CREATOR; and
LOVE THE ONLY LAW.

Mind manifests itself through Thought, which externalizes and individualizes the creations of Mind, whatever they may be. They may not be visible to us, but they are real.

Thoughts become absolute things, and having once been formed and sent out, live on and on indefinitely. They fill certain belts of the unseen, they pass and re-pass, jostling together, and a certain class on the lower animal plane war upon each other, giving rise to much mental suffering in the cases of persons of extremely nervous and psychic temperaments. Somewhere, somebody sang,

"Thoughts are things,
  Having being, breath and wings."

Father Ryan has expressed it better than I can.

"They wear holy veils on their faces;
  Their footsteps can scarcely be heard;
They pass through the valley, like virgins,
  Too pure for the touch of a word."

In the spiritual darkness of the present, there has developed in the mind of the race a belief in a power outside of God, and more potent, which man has named Evil; also a belief in a substance, other than Spirit, which he calls Matter. Both formulas are erroneous and the outgrowth of misunderstanding, and can be dissipated, with all their evil effects, as he becomes familiar with and lives up to the foundation principles herein laid down.

Man, as man, cannot continue to exist without a religion; it must form the basis of his character. He must recognize a Supreme Power. He must worship—or GO OUT!

When I say religion, I do not refer to forms or ceremonies or external rites, but religion in its truest sense, in the perfect form which our Master laid down in His Sermon on the Mount.

We are endeavoring in this brotherhood to demonstrate the fact that the religion of Christ can be made the guiding principle in every-day life. Not religion consisting alone of a worship of the Supreme Being, but one embracing also the highest grades of ethics—that commands us to love our enemies, to do good to those who hate us, to give, expecting nothing in return, to deal justly, to judge not, to condemn not, and to forgive as we would be forgiven. The experience of half a century in this colony has proven that Christ's religion is a safe guide to go by.

According to sacred historians the commencement of all the disasters that have befallen the race and planet was the evolution in Man of an independent mind and will; outside of, and in opposition to, the Creative Mind. He went into business on his own responsibility and without capital. His self-constituted outside mind was not composed of the true Substance—the divine mental atoms. It is a counterfeit, and all that it sees, feels or imagines is false.

This mind belongs exclusively to the animal man. It has no knowledge of or attraction toward the divine; the thoughts generated and sent out by it never rise higher than the fleshly demands. These form a dense and murky mental atmosphere near the earth, powerful enough to hypnotize the entire race, producing what we know as race belief, so that on many points all men are of one mind and thought.

The average individual thinks and believes along certain lines just as the world does, and feels uncomfortable at the suggestion of any new thought; feels oppressed at any mental agitation above the average strata. To talk to one thus fettered of a higher and more healthy region of thought, of unexplored kingdoms in the invisible, is to speak to him in an unknown tongue; he does not concern himself about the invisible, in fact does not believe in anything that cannot be recognized through his five senses. Such, in fact, never think, they simply believe what the strongest party believes.

This fleshly mind is that disobedient, faithless, selfish, Godless mind now controlling the world. It governs all business transactions, marriages, family relations and general society. It loves after its own fashion what belongs to it, and often deals generously with its own, because it is giving to itself, gratifying its "myness." "These are my children, this is my home, this is my wife," rarely taking thought of the thousands who are homeless, breadless, dying in want. It gives in charity where it brings the applause of the world, which is the only god it can comprehend. In this mind exists all passions, prejudices, crimes, cruelty, greed, hatred, licentiousness and murder. Here also exists the sense life, the belief in pain, disease and death.

St. Paul says of this mind, "For to be carnally minded is death. Because the carnal mind is enmity against God; for it is not subject to the law of God, neither indeed can be." "To be carnally minded is death, but to be spiritually minded is life and peace." Paul's spiritual mind is the divine Mind, and if it be permitted the ascendncy it will control all things. It is that power in man that makes him a son of God. It was this Mind in Christ that performed all miracles and works of magic; turned water into wine, multiplied the loaves and fishes, stilled the tempest, healed the sick, cleansed the leper, and raised the dead. That was the "higher magic."

Man to fulfill his destiny must become master of that magic, must control his thoughts, must not only be capable of protecting himself from the baleful effects of the evil thoughts of those on the animal plane, but must possess a commanding influence over the baser elements in the mental atmosphere about him. That is, he must control the masses and mould their thoughts for good. He can do it, in a degree, if he is governed by his divine Mind, for that is the Power which commands all things. It said, "Let there be light."

Some years since, I was present at an anti-slavery meeting in a large eastern city where the most powerful man of his time was to speak. An immense crowd had assembled, composed of every conceivable order of mind; a large portion of which held the most antagonistic views regarding the anti-slavery cause, as well as a bitter hatred toward the speaker. It was a mental atmosphere largely on the animal plane. It was like a huge powder magazine requiring but a spark to bring an explosion.

The speaker arose, stepped forward, and laid his hand upon the desk, stood silent and motionless for a moment expressing a majesty that he alone of all the men of the day possessed. He commenced speaking, rather slowly at first, as was his custom, making not the slightest gesture. Presently he began to pour forth eloquent words, once heard never forgotten, kindling in the breasts of the devoted lovers of justice and freedom a fire that never smouldered or died out.

The low brutal thought element began to vibrate and seethe with suppressed rage and excitement; then to lash; then the storm burst! Hisses, howls and execrations were poured out against the cause and the speaker. The tumult was for the time deafening.

To one unaccustomed to gatherings of that nature a riot appeared imminent. I looked over the audience to see if there were any movements toward quelling the disturbance, but no one moved in that direction. Then I looked toward the speaker.

He had not even stirred, but stood perfectly motionless, with that firm right hand still resting on the desk where he had first laid it. He stood like a god and faced that belligerent element, with a countenance unruffled and calm and a certain masterful expression that was indescribable. The fury began to subside, order was restored, and the house became quiet without a word of protest from any quarter.

The speaker took up his subject just where he had left off, without a comment or change of voice or countenance, and continued holding the attention of the entire audience with ever-deeping interest and without a dissenting voice to the close. He was master of that higher magic. He said to that turbulent sea of brutal thought, Peace, be still. And it obeyed him; just as the storm on the Sea of Galilee two thousand years ago obeyed the commands of the Master Magician.

What was true of those commanding minds is equally true of all who are controlled by their divine Mind and will.

We must not forget that there are many stratas of thought. All thought originating in the minds of men influences in a silent way the minds of all other men that come in contact with them.

All books, although unread, influence the mind of the race for good or evil, according to the nature of the thoughts embodied in them. Thoughts of hatred, animal passions, jealousy or anger, although not expressed, arouse kindred thoughts in others on the same plane; so that what was merely the thought of crime in one may come into expression through another, who yet would never have thought of the wrong. Crimes of all descriptions are contagious. They are in the air as much so as diseases. On the other hand so likewise are good thoughts, kindness, love and mercy. They are on a higher plane, but we can have them if we reach high enough. Thoughts rise according to their specific gravity.

To think of the divine source of love, is to send the thoughts to the center of all Good. That in the highest sense is prayer. The mental atoms have been to the bosom of the Infinite, and return laden with divine love strong to heal and bless. To strongly desire the well-being of another is to pray for that one.

Prayer does not consist in many and eloquent words. All elevated and unselfish thoughts are prayers. The high and pure aspirations of all lovers of the race have formed a mental zone above the atmosphere created by the carnal or fleshly mind. In this elevated belt of thought is stored the wisdom of every grand soul that has ever inhabited our planet. Nothing is ever lost, nor is there anything new.

We, if we desire, can have access to this mighty storehouse where all the wisdom of the past and future awaits our demands. We have only to come to the consciousness of the Supreme Mind within us to become possessors of the vast riches in store for the seeker after truth.

The wise Egyptian, Balthazar, was doubtless very familiar with this elevated region of thought. He says, "There is a kingdom on the earth, though not of it; a kingdom wider than the bounds of the earth, though they were rolled together as finest gold and spread by the beating of hammers. Its existence is a fact, as our hearts are facts, and we journey through it from birth to death without seeing it; nor shall any man see it till he hath first known his own soul; for this kingdom is not for him, but for his soul. And in its dominions there is glory such as hath not entered into imagination—original, incomparable, impossible of increase. Nor shall any man see it till he hath first known his own soul." This soul of man is his divine Mind. He is to enlarge it. He is to earn his divinity. He is to accumulate all the wisdom of the ages in order that he also may become one among the hosts of Gods who fashion the objective universe.

Mankind has for the time lost his focalization with the Supreme central Mind. That is why we need religious education now especially.

"Let him that is endued with Mind, know himself to be immortal; and that the cause of death is the love of the body.

"But as many souls of men, as do not admit or entertain the Mind for their Governor, do suffer the same thing that the soul of unreasonable living things.

"And as brute beasts, they are angry without reason, and they desire without reason, and never cease, nor are satisfied with Evil.

"Therefore hath God set the Mind over these, as a Revenger and Reprover of them."

—Hermes in "Divine Pymander."

Father Hyacinth smilingly took his departure, and Brother Frederick stepped forward, introduced the new members of the class to those of the brotherhood present. One splendid-looking man, whom I afterward learned to know as Brother Paul, rose from among the group and welcomed us to the "Home" and the fellowship with the "Brothers" and "Sisters" of the Mystic Circle. The entire group arose and smilingly bowed to us; then dispersed in various directions.

To one Sister was assigned the duty of entertaining our party until the dinner hour. To our family group were added ten new members, men and women from various portions of the country, beside a scientist from Germany, who had a most singular way of studying people through his glasses, causing them to feel that he was analyzing the component parts of their etheric substance or some such thing.

As we passed out of the house, he dropped back to my side and said that he had just come from a visit to Tesla's laboratory,—wherever that may be, I did not inquire, I was too busy in taking in my new and novel surroundings to care to talk upon science. I gradually made my way toward the front of the group, near the Sister, to hear her explanations of the colony, a subject of greater interest to me just then than anything else.

One could well imagine oneself in a town, so numerous were the buildings, and grouped with such system and order, with regular streets, electricity, water supplies, and telephones. All this, remember, is located up on a mountain side; it was literally "a city set upon a hill." It stood in the midst of a grove of the grandest trees that I have ever seen. The Home was of great size and massiveness, something after the style of the old English castles. The buildings for animals, the storing of farm produce, the packing of fruits, manufacturing purposes, electricity, etc., were of the same architectural design and finish. The entire town was built of the native stone, of a soft light-gray color, with a fine grain and very durable.

The Sister who escorted us over the place, informed us that there were five thousand acres in the plantation. That there were three hundred acres devoted to orange groves, now in full bearing; three hundred to cherries, five hundred and fifty to grapes, fifty to strawberries, and five hundred to plums and peaches, and about twenty-five to garden produce for the family, including one hundred acres to black and red raspberries.

This Sister also said, with a show of pride, that they milked one hundred and fifty cows, all of the choicest Jersey breed, and that their butter brought the highest market price; that they had twenty-five horses on the place, with the necessary equipments; that their system of irrigation was the most perfect in the State, and that they had just completed arrangements for the manufacturing of ice, which would enable them to make a perfect success of their creamery, as well as the storing of fruit.

"Our buildings are all lighted by electricity, as you see," our guide continued, "and the most interesting part of the whole matter is," here her face lighted up, "that the planning and the entire work has been accomplished by members of the brotherhood. We have in our family four as fine artists as there are in the world, who were very celebrated before they came to us. There are two painters, one sculptor and one architect—three men and one woman. The woman is our finest painter. She has done all the large paintings for the Home; those pieces in the chapel were hers. The painting of the walls and other decorations were the work of Brothers Andrew and James, so that through the finished skill of the Brothers and Sisters we have in our Home not only solid comfort, but real artistic finish." Here she smiled, showing two dimples and a mouth full of perfect teeth.

"What number have you in your fraternity?" asked Angela.

"There are five hundred life members, taking old and young," replied the Sister. "They are not all in the Home at this present time. A number of the more gifted and experienced are out in the world, teaching in different portions or the country. It is not known that they are connected with this community. There is never any proselyting done by the members of the brotherhood, as only such can unite with us as are prepared to live the strict life of self-sacrifice and seclusion."

"Where are all the children?" inquired a Boston man, who had been deeply absorbed in all that had been said.

"Well, at the present time we have no very young children," answered the Sister. "The youngest ones, from ten to fifteen, have grown up in the colony—they came in quite young; some of them were babies. But we shall soon have more children, as there are several families coming who have quite young members."

"You said that families came into this association, husbands and their wives; are there no children born in the Home?" I ventured to ask.

"No, there are no children born here; you will understand that celibacy is the foundation tenet in our creed," replied the Sister.

"Then, how do you expect to increase in number and become permanent?" I persisted.

"Oh, by voluntary contribution from the outer world," smilingly answered our guide.

"Will not this community, like many others of a similar character, be likely to disorganize and disband in time?" asked a young man, who had the air of a divinity student.

"We think not," replied the Sister. "Our fraternity started with less than a half dozen families, over fifty years ago. It has steadily increased in numbers and prosperity. In all of their experience there have been but five life members who have withdrawn because they could not adapt their lives to that of the community."

Here we were startled by the ringing of a loud but sweet-toned bell hanging in the tower of Home building.

"That is the signal for dinner," said our charming escort, turning and smiling upon her eager, enthusiastic company. "Come up this way," she continued, as she, with her elastic step and graceful robe, preceded us up the broad steps to the main entrance of the Home.

On the porch we halted to look down over the valley—over thousands of acres of rich and highly cultivated land; over orange groves; over orchards of plum, peach and cherry trees; over fields of grapes and strawberries; and, over and above all, such sunshine as can be seen nowhere else under heaven. As we narrowed our vision, and brought it up to the lawn in front of the Home, we were greeted by a sight that must delight all lovers of flowers. Such a wealth of roses as no one could imagine unless he had been in this country and witnessed for himself the manner in which nature arrays herself in this her bridal season.

Annie came to me in great excitement, shocked that Brother Paul should have introduced her to two full-blooded Africans. I studied the two men as we passed on. They were as black as ebony, but each had the bearing of a king, and the white surplices, and the dignity with which they bore themselves, made them a most conspicuous and attractive study. They were given the honor of showing us to our seats at the table, which they did with such grace and dignity that even Annie was filled with admiration; she, leaning over to me, whispered, "Well,

I never could believe that a darkey could be so splendid looking. It is just because they are up here." I observed that a peculiar deference was shown these men, the cause of which I learned later.

On our way to the dining room I took a hasty survey of the interior of the building on the first floor. I noticed that the floors were all of hard wood, and highly polished, with here and there handsome rugs. The walls were of a golden tint, without paper or figures of any kind, but hanging upon them were many elegant paintings and choice steel engravings. Wherever the eye rested there were evidences of refinement; in the rich furniture, rare works of art, and bits of choice sculpture. Many of the families, the Sister had told us, had not only brought their wealth to the colony, but had also brought many of the rare things that had adorned their homes in other countries.

As we entered the dining room I was astonished at not only the size, but its curious shape. It was semi-circular in form, and supplied with large windows which flooded the room with light.

In this room were a large number of tables, at each of which could be seated twenty persons. They were made of some dark wood, mahogany I should judge, and polished until they shone like mirrors. The chairs were also of some dark wood. There were no cloths, but here and there upon the tables pretty doilies for the large dishes. In the center of each table was a flat oval dish, in which was a beautiful variety of growing fern, a native of the mountains here.

Although everything was on so large a scale, yet there was an air of delicacy and refinement extremely pleasing. The china, glass and silver, though not of an expensive kind, had evidently been selected with a view to artistic effect. There was a perfect uniformity in the arrangements. The tables were all laid with care and everything was immaculately clean.

The fruit dishes were heaped with strawberries, oranges and bananas; and scattered about the tables in profusion were glass pitchers filled with rich yellow cream and milk, with a generous supply of sugar at hand. No meats were served; but there were eggs in great abundance, prepared in various ways, with a variety of delicious vegetables cooked in the most appetizing manner, butter and cream entering largely into their preparation. And the bread and butter—well, Annie said that it was "meat fit for the gods," whoever they might be.

In the serving of this meal there were no attendants; nobody entered or left the room during the time. No one arose from the tables. At each table a Brother cut the bread on a large carved wooden platter. Everyone assisted in the serving, and yet there was no confusion or noise. The Sisters served the fruit.

The whole arrangement of that room, the laying of the tables, the nature and delicacy of the food, the manner of serving, the general air of good breeding that prevailed, the courtesy displayed by one to another, is a picture indelibly impressed upon my mind as one of the most perfect things in all my experience. I had always had an aversion to eating with a crowd. Any noise or uncouth manners at table were sufficient to destroy all desire for food that I may have had. But Lord Chesterfield himself could have found no fault with the table manners of these people. There was no moving of the feet or chairs.

One thing impressed me greatly, and that was their peculiar, low, deliberate manner of speaking, together with a certain musical quality of voice most pleasing. I had noticed this peculiarity in Angela's manner of speech. It was so marked in her case, that, in traveling or in crowds, when she would speak strangers would mahogany I should judge, and polished until they shone like mirrors. The chairs were also of some dark wood. There were no cloths, but here and there upon the tables pretty doilies for the large dishes. In the center of each table was a flat oval dish, in which was a beautiful variety of growing fern, a native of the mountains here.

Although everything was on so large a scale, yet there was an air of delicacy and refinement extremely pleasing. The china, glass and silver, though not of an expensive kind, had evidently been selected with a view to artistic effect. There was a perfect uniformity in the arrangements. The tables were all laid with care and everything was immaculately clean.

The fruit dishes were heaped with strawberries, oranges and bananas; and scattered about the tables in profusion were glass pitchers filled with rich yellow cream and milk, with a generous supply of sugar at hand. No meats were served; but there were eggs in great abundance. prepared in various ways, with a variety of delicious vegetables cooked in the most appetizing manner, butter and cream entering largely into their preparation. And the bread and butter—well, Annie said that it was "meat fit for the gods," whoever they might be.

In the serving of this meal there were no attendants; nobody entered or left the room during the time. No one arose from the tables. At each table a Brother cut the bread on a large carved wooden platter. Everyone assisted in the serving, and yet there was no confusion or noise. The Sisters served the fruit.

The whole arrangement of that room, the laying of the tables, the nature and delicacy of the food, the manner of serving, the general air of good breeding that prevailed, the courtesy displayed by one to another, is a picture indelibly impressed upon my mind as one of the most perfect things in all my experience. I had always had an aversion to eating with a crowd. Any noise or uncouth manners at table were sufficient to destroy all desire for food that I may have had. But Lord Chesterfield himself could have found no fault with the table manners of these people. There was no moving of the feet or chairs.

One thing impressed me greatly, and that was their peculiar, low, deliberate manner of speaking, together with a certain musical quality of voice most pleasing. I had noticed this peculiarity in Angela's manner of speech. It was so marked in her case, that, in traveling or in crowds, when she would speak strangers would turn and look at her. And now, in comparison with those about us, Annie's voice and mine appeared to be strung up•on a metallic key that grated terribly. I had never noticed it before, although John had told us that we talked too loud.

These people ate as deliberately as they talked; they exhibited no haste in anything. They displayed an air of cheerfulness and an ease of manner surprising to me when I remembered that the Sister had told us that many members of the community had not been off the plantation in fifteen years.

Father Hyacinth was the principal speaker at dinner. He had just returned from an extended trip through the various fruit-growing regions, and his talk was upon the different methods of crating, storing and shipping fruit. This subject appeared to interest the entire company. Then, too, the speaker had such a charming manner of relating his experience with the people in the various localities which he had visited. One could well imagine himself at some great banquet, so leisurely and comfortably was the whole affair conducted.

The serving and the partaking of that meal gave me an insight into the character of the people that nothing but time and a close relationship in other ways could have done. As passed this meal, so passed all others during our stay of many months with this most remarkable and fascinating band of recluses.

I found that they did not believe in making slaves of themselves, there being no incentive to individuals to amass wealth, as every man and woman had secured to them, not only a delightful home, guarantee of care and attention in case of sickness and in old age; but a certain annuity from the Corporation, which John informed me was on as strict a basis as the United States Government.

As time passed, I discovered that the members never labored to exceed six hours a day, and that only during the season of gathering, storing and shipping fruit; at all other times four or five hours were the rule. Everything is done to make the home life attractive and delightful, and their efforts have been successful.

This community is a world within itself. Their landed possessions were full of resources, which this ingenious people have developed to an astonishing perfection.

Through Annie's skill in shorthand I am enabled to give a tolerable digest of the strange and wonderful doctrines taught and believed, yes, and lived up to, by this singular school of Mystics.

CHAPTER II.

Benares, California, April 15th.

This morning the new members of the class, twelve in number, breakfasted with the family, and were ready at half past six to start on a tour of inspection and study of this most wonderful country and community.

We have been here over a week, and yet have investigated but a small portion of this immense enterprise. One or two of the Brothers or Sisters usually accompany the party in their rounds as a matter of courtesy, as well as to give information. Pleasant, high-toned manners are displayed by this people at all times and under all circumstances. A Brother never meets one without lifting his hat, or a Sister without a bow and a smile. This show of deference and respect is manifested toward the least in importance in the colony. I discovered early that unusual deference was always shown those of alien blood, the African and Japanese members.

We had learned that there were two excursions to this resort each month, commencing in April and continuing until July. They came from the various towns along the line of the Northern Pacific Railroad, occasionally one from San Francisco.

The Brother, a Japanese, who was our escort this morning informed us that today was the date for the San Francisco excursion, which would reach the plantation at twelve o'clock. He said that refreshments would be served as soon as the guests arrived, that the tables would be laid on the lawn under the trees. I now observed that several of the Brothers were engaged in unloading folding chairs and tables from a large furniture van.

We were informed that Brothers Paul and Frederick had the management of these enterprises. That the excursionists often numbered two and three hundred, and that the sales of fruit, honey, cheese, butter, eggs, etc., were at times enormous.

The refreshments were gratuitous, and the ride to and from the station free also. Our guide said, laughingly, "When those city people get up here, and take in this mountain air, they get so hungry that it sometimes looks doubtful about our finding enough food on the plantation to feed them; but our band plays during the meal, and the music somehow seems to satisfy them. We always give them our choicest music, and you know what that is," he said, turning to a professor of music from Berlin.

We had discovered that among the members of the colony there were musicians of a very superior order, both in the line of vocal and instrumental music. To make the most and best of every faculty for good is the leading principle of this peculiar people, so that those displaying talents of any order were encouraged to cultivate them, the best teachers and facilities being employed to this end.

There was an orchestra composed of eight of the Sisters, who played upon stringed instruments, and who gave one of the most perfect entertainments to which I have ever listened. Brother Rameses being their leader and insrtuctor. There was also a well organized military band that, for an hour each evening, out on the lawn, discoursed the choicest music of the great composers, from Chopin down.

The attraction for me in all their music was the performance of their principal violinist, Brother Rameses, an Austrian by birth. He was of massive proportions and commanding presence—more like Wilhelmj than any one else I had ever seen. There was a silent power about the man that appeared to elevate those that looked at him, and as he slowly and gracefully drew the bow over the strings of his instrument, one could not help feeling a regret that all the world could not listen to his inspiring and elevating music.

The professor from Berlin, who was up here in the mountains for his health, pronounced the entire musical department of the colony as perfect in every detail.

I learned that the violinist was on the program for the day. This concert usually occupied not more than an hour, so that the visitors could have time to investigate the working of the institution.

As this was the morning for the lesson, when the great clock struck the quarter to nine we all turned our steps toward the Home. One of the new students, a man from Boston, walking along by my side, said, "Is there anywhere on earth another such a spot or such a people? It is all so new and strange to me, yes, and perfect, that I want to stay here the remainder of my life."

I looked up into his frank, smiling countenance and noted the faint glow of health that had been from day to day slowly deepening on his cheeks, and said, "You are less excitable and much more harmonious than when you first came. I think you may be trusted to stay," I added with gravity.

"Well, then, allow me the privilege of sitting next to you in the class this morning," he said smilingly, as we entered the chapel.

We took our seats, and after our long walk in the exhilarating mountain air the holy quiet of this room appeared to fall like a benediction on all.

John, who was always seated at my right, came in with Annie, and, taking his accustomed place beside me, said, in a low voice, "I wish you to give your undivided attention to the subject of the lesson this morning, it is of importance to all. There are certain truths which you need to understand."

"I will," I replied, looking into his grand face and wondering why they did not make them all like John. Then I closed my eyes, and listening to the music and singing wandered in thought away back to those remote ages when men were supposed to have been angelic beings, and I wondered if they were really any better than some of the human family I knew at the present time.

Presently I was aroused from my reverie by the voice of Father Hyacinth announcing the subjcet of the morning's lesson, that old and hackneyed story of the Creation of Man and our Planet.

The Boston man leaned over, and whispering to me, said, "I want you to watch me, and pinch me or stick pins in me, for I shall go to sleep; I have heard all I care to about the creation business, and unless your preacher can trump up something new in this line I would rather pick oranges."

"You mean that you would rather eat them," I snapped out, drawing myself away from his side unable to conceal my disgust at his levity.

At this point Father Hyacinth commenced his lesson and I forgot my irritation and impatience in the fascination of the speaker and the subject.

"Every man is appointed by God to know and to contemplate."

—Pythagoras.

"There is no other true religion than to meditate on the universe and give thanks to the Creator. * * * * How happily constituted and near to the Gods is humanity! In joining himself to the divine, man disdains that which he has in him of the earthly; he connects himself by a bond of love to all other beings, and thereby feels himself necessary to the universal order. He contemplates heaven; and in this happy middle sphere, in which he is placed, he loves all that is below him; he is beloved by all that is above."

—Hermes.

"Let us realize it again and again—man is the lord of all that exists; his crown of thorns is his crown of glory. That which elevates man above all other beings is his capacity for suffering, and the consequent power of asking for its extinction absolutely and forever."

—Mohini M. Chatterji.

SECOND LESSON.

THE CREATION OF MAN AND OUR PLANET.

The study of the creation of the race and the planetary system is not as a rule considered of much importance to the average individual. It is so remote from anything on the plane of his daily life, that it appears of trifling value in comparison to the present existence. Very few can see any relation between the celestial Man and the man of today, in fact scarcely believe there ever was a celestial Man, and planet to match—indeed rarely think anything concerning the matter. Were it not a fixed fact in the philosophy of life that the Thought of the race not only moulds the character and nature of the race, but also the planet down to its lowest kingdom, we would not have the courage to bring forward so unsavory a topic.

The animal or natural man, as he exists today, has little or no capacity to comprehend the character of the divine Being or Power or celestial Hierarchy which he has been taught to call

God. There is, however, deep in the higher nature of humanity, a dim sense of a Supreme Power; and in the history of the world it has been only those who have followed that instinct that have reached any degree of satisfaction in their labors of life.

Now as a crowning statement in our proposition we declare that the real Man is an offspring of the divine Central Mind and possesses in embryo all of the potentialities of the divine Parent. He is not merely a demonstration of, but the demonstrator of the Central Intelligence, and one with the celestial hosts of Gods whose mission it is to develop the ideas and plans of the Central Architect or Mind. "I have said, Ye are Gods, and all of you children of the Most High," said the mystic David.

That wise Egyptian, Hermes, who lived, thought and wrote centuries before David's time, who like Paul was conveyed away into Paradise and heard, "Things spoken which is not possible for man to relate," says, "Man is a divine living thing, and is not to be compared to any brute beast that lives upon earth, but to them that are above in heaven, that are called Gods. Wherefore we must be bold to say, That an earthly man, is a mortal God; and that the heavenly God, is an immortal Man."

It will be difficult for those seeing only the degraded side of human nature to accept the statement of man's divinity. I am aware there is a crookedness manifested that does not harmonize with the theory of the race having been created in the likeness of God. But I take the position that this forbidding outside aspect is only temporary. Man in his central life is still divine. He cannot help himself. Because God exists, and is eternal, Man must exist eternally. God being the infinite, the divine Central Life, could create nothing unlike himself and there is but the one Substance from which all things are made.

"Thus saith the Lord, the holy one of Israel, Ask me of things to come concerning my sons, and concerning the work of my hands—I have made the earth and created Man upon it; I, even my hands, have stretched out the heavens, and all their hosts have I commanded."

"And God said, Let us make man in our image, after our likeness; and let them have dominion." According to this statement God did not operate alone. "Let US make man,"—who was US?

From a careful study of all ancient and sacred history, we learn that there are, in the domains of the Supreme Overmind, celestial Hierarchies or orders of Gods, who in the scheme of creation perform the behest of the Supreme, making His thoughts manifest. According to the most occult authority, Christ was the leading intelligence in our circle, and through His creative fiat our solar system and Man came into objective being.

"For the Father of all things, the Mind, being Life and Light, brought forth Man, like unto himself, whom he loved ; for he was all beauteous, having the Image of his Father.

"For the Mind being God, Male and Female, Life and Light, brought forth by his Word ; another Mind, the Workman ; which being God of the Fire and the Spirit, fashioned and formed seven other Governors, which in their circles contain the Sensible World"

—Hermes.

There are doubtless many circles and great assemblages of celestial beings sitting in council on the momentous work of the evolving and objectifying of suns, systems, and races of men. As there are myriads of glowing suns in that belt of light known to us as the "Milky Way," so there are myriads of Godlike beings who come and go, doing the work of manifesting the thoughts and plans of the great Central Mind of our spiritual universe.

Creation was not the work of past ages alone, but is an ever-present movement of divine Mind. The "wheel of life" is ceaseless disintegration and creation, ever evolving new forms from the old, without the loss or destruction of one particle of the divine Substance.

But for the present we are interested only in our own solar system, and especially in the history of the creation of our race and planet.

To be explicit: Christ was the creator of the objective man and this world. We are therefore His creation, and that is the reason it is so imperative that mankind should come into understanding of and at-onement with Him. The objective man cannot exist without Him. The soul is doomed that will not recognize the Christ, because He is the Light and Life of all souls, and to persistently shut away that Light is for them to eventually go out in utter darkness—to become disintegrated; to lose their objectivity.

This teaching presents Christ in a new light, and brings Him into closer relationship to our humanity, and explains why He, of all the Gods, came to the world to redeem the race and restore all things. "He came to redeem His own, and complete His work." Our interpretation of the first chapter of St. John will unveil much that appears mysterious and irreconcilable, and out of which has grown widely divergent opinions and creeds.

In the first chapter of St. John the Logos—or Word—always signifies the Christ. "In the beginning was the Word, and the Word was with God, and the Word was God,"—or "a" God. "The same was in the beginning with God. And the Word was made flesh, and dwelt among men, and we beheld His glory, as of the only begotten of the Father, full of grace and truth. Which was born, not of blood, nor of the will of flesh, nor of the will of man, but of God. In Him was life; and the life was the light of men. All things were made by Him; and without Him was not anything made that was made. He was in the world, and the world was made by Him, and the world knew Him not. He came to his own domains and yet His own people received Him not."

We have Christ's own words: "My Father worketh hitherto, and I work. For the Father loveth the Son, and showeth Him all things that Himself doeth; and He will show Him greater works than these, that you may marvel. For what things soever He doeth, these also doeth the Son likewise. As the Father has life in Himself; so He gives also to the Son to have life in Himself. I am the way, the truth and the life; no man cometh unto the Father but by Me."

Almost His last utterances were these: "And now, O Father, glorify Thou Me, with thine own self with the glory which I had with Thee before the world was. For Thou lovedst Me before the foundation of the world."

Paul says: "There is one God, the Father, OF WHOM are all things, and we IN HIM; and one Lord Jesus Christ, BY WHOM are all things, and we BY HIM."

And again, in the first chapter of Hebrews, he says: "God * * * hath in these last days spoken unto us by His Son, whom He hath appointed heir of all things, by whom also He made the worlds; who being the brightness of His glory, and the express image of His person, and making manifest all things by the word of His power."

In the religious teachings of the world, man has been represented as so vile and far removed from the divine that to reinstate him would appear impossible. So long has he been taught that he was utterly degraded and debased in both soul and body that he has grown to believe the story, and has materialized conditions suitable to such a state of mind. In order to redeem him we must change this manner of thinking and teaching.

"God created Man in His own image, in the image of God created He him. And God saw everything that He had made, and, behold, it was very good." From this we perceive that man, being in the divine likeness, must, like his source, possess infinite possibilities, perfections and duration. He has not the power to destroy anything created by the divine Mind.

He has for the time lost sight of his divine nature; has forgotten his first estate, as the aged and infirm often lose the remembrances of the scenes and events of their childhood and youth; the spiritual consciousness has become obscured through the sense life.

The divine Mind in man is endued with all spiritual understanding, and as he enters the realms of that Mind he comes into consciousness of what appears to the worldly mind so strange and mysterious. Christ, endeavoring to instruct the ignorant and stupid crowd that daily followed His footsteps, said, "Are your hearts stupified? Having eyes, do you not see? and having ears, do you not hear? and do you not recollect?" Appealing to their spiritual consciousness of truths hidden beneath the heavy burden of the fleshly memory.

"Our life is but a sleep, and a forgetting,
  The soul that rises in us,—our life-star—
Hath had elsewhere its setting,
  And cometh from afar."

Time, like all of man's inventions, is a weighty and oppressive thing. In our present narrowed mental condition we cannot grasp the idea of the vast periods required to restore the life of our planet and its inhabitants. We try to sense in a bewildered way the slow and silent process.

We can form but a dim conception of the angelic Man. We are told that he was formed in the "image of God," the divine Creator, whose Nature is Love, whose Substance is Spirit, whose creative Power is Mind; who is unlimited,—from everlasting unto everlasting,—all-seeing, all-knowing. And Man was created of His Substance and in His likeness; and our Guide said, "Be ye perfect, even as your Father in heaven is perfect."

The reason that we cannot comprehend the nature and power of God, and Christ, is because we do not understand Man, his creative genius, his reasoning power, his marvelous insight into hidden forces.

The creation of a planet and a race of men

would not appear so incomprehensible if we stopped for a moment to consider the wonderful creative ability of man. The planning and building of our great cities, our navies, our commercial, electric, telegraphic and steam faci'ities, all evolved through man's inventive and creative genius; the architect and the artist conceiving the ideas, which are submitted to others competent to externalize them. One need only to watch Tripler's experiments with his "liquified air;" or more wonderful still, Tesla's demonstration of the "electric life of the universe;" to comprehend how a higher grade of mind might be able to evolve from the cosmic ether, which contains the essence of all shapes, an objective world and its inhabitants.

The men of our present day, possessing but ordinary mental capacity, have opened a door into hidden forces, back of which lies a latent and almighty Power awaiting the command of the human race to evolve so-called miracles far beyond our present comprehension. The majority of the race can form no more conception of the order of Mind through which a planet and a race of men could be evolved, than I, having no knowledge of astronomy, could understand the velocity of the planets in their revolutions around their centers, or be prepared to tell when the comets, meteoric showers or eclipses are due, or of the Martian's mode of irrigation.

Evidently, the divine idea was to give expression to "individuality;" to develop objective life, "create forms." "The earth was without form and void, and darkness was upon the face of the deep." Our planet had not yet assumed shape. "The face of the deep" was the vast ocean of cosmic, or spiritual Substance, from which are evolved all forms of objective life.

The MIND—the image of Christ—in man, is the Power that creates all the marvels of the objective worlds. Not only the vegetable, but also the animal kingdoms come forth at his bidding; all of the glories of architecture, art, literature and science—in brief, he has created the objective world.

A limited observation of what we call the world of nature would be sufficient to convince the thoughtful student of the truth of this theory. All that has ever come to the race, by way of advancement or comfort from the lower kingdoms, has been the result of man's intelligent effort keeping pace with his demands.

As illustrations, we will take the present conditions of those countries that man has in a measure forsaken, which were once the pride and glory of the world. The Pyramids of Egypt, silently brooding over the wastes of sand, could they but speak, would confirm this apparently extravagant statement. Where is now the glory of Egypt? of Phoenicia? of Babylonia? of Assyria? Where is Thebes, with her grand and massive architecture and her groves of orange, citron and olive? Where are the Hanging Gardens of Babylon? Alas! all the marvels of art and science have disappeared like shadows, and what we are wont to call Nature fades out and is gone when man withdraws his love and fostering care.

The evolving of our planet out of the cosmic Substance, the putting forth on our globe of the various kingdoms, is controlled by the Mind of Man. The multiplied eons during which our world has revolved in its ocean of ether is of secondary interest to us. Man is the crowning glory of the whole creation. To know Man is to know God.

The primeval Man would not be so attractive to us, but from the fact that his existence and destiny is intimately linked with ours; we have walked hand in hand with him down the slopes of time, and we cannot know ourselves until we have come into understanding of his origin and nature. We are but a branch of that great family that left the Father's house on their tour of investigation ages and ages ago, when the morning stars sang together.

We will briefly review the early history of our race as far back as there is any record, beyond that, doubtless for countless ages, the Adamic race existed in the radiant atmosphere of a sinless world, where selfishness, disease and death were unknown.

We can form no accurate conception of the nature or condition of the inhabitants, or our planet, at that time. From very ancient records we find this statement: "God made not death; neither hath He pleasure in the destruction of the living. For he created all things that they might have their being; and the generations of the world were healthful, and there was no poison or destruction in them, nor the kingdom of death upon the earth." *

From Vedantic authorities we learn that man was even in the second and third eras an ethereal being, and that the exhalations of his body were deliciously fragrant; and that all animals at that period were like trees, flowers and plants, most fragrant." "It is next to impossible," says this authority, "to give a true conception of the human beings who once walked this earth; its early possessors. They can only

* Book of Wisdom.

be realized by the seer, and conceived by those whose imaginative powers are of a very high degree." *

It is generally supposed that the first and second chapters of Genesis relate to the one creation, and the decided difference in the two histories has led to great complications and confusion, because of the unlikeness of the two creations.

In the first chapter it is stated: "God created Man in His own image. And God saw everything that He had made, and, behold, it was very good."

The second chapter evidently relates to a period in the experience of the race and planet widely remote from the first history. The first creation was the spiritual Man, in the likeness of the Most High. The angelic Man not yet having entered into objective life.

In the second chapter we find, "The Lord God," who was given the mission from the Father to bring into material life the race and the planet (God being the Father, the Lord God being the Son), "formed man of the dust of the ground, and breathed into his nostrils the breath of life; and man became a living soul." This is not a creation—"Became" a living soul. To be-

* Fragments of Forgotten History.

come, is to pass from one state or condition into another, assuming new qualities and offices.

"Formed man of the dust of the ground." this symbolizes a more material state, as we call it; but more properly speaking the race and planet had entered into objective life, although Man was still a sinless and angelic being, and the world was as yet in a perfect state.

"He breathed into his nostrils the breath of life, and man became a living soul." This soul is something that has been given to the spiritual Man who was created in God's image, a necessary Helper in his search after knowledge. The soul represents an individual mind which will enable Man to gather up and store away the knowledge gained from the varied experiences of his numerous lives. This soul or mind reaches out, and gathers in all the modes of divine operation; dips down into the lowest—if there be any lowest—where the spiritual Man could not go, that it may receive instruction concerning the mysterious process of creation. In this soul is locked a knowledge of all things.

You will keep before you the fact that soul and Spirit are two distinct entities, having widely different missions to fulfill. After working out its destiny, the soul, rich in the experience of its numerous lives, will come into at-onement with the Spirit, thus completing the destiny of man and making of him a God.

The soul or mind is an aggregation of innumerable consciousnesses which, when polarized, becomes as an effulgent sun the center of man's life, as the Supreme Mind is the center of the universe. This mind grows. It becomes. It expands. It can sin; and IT CAN DIE.

But the Spirit in man is sinless and deathless. It knows no change, is in the likeness of the Supreme Father, the Jehovah Elohim.

It was Christ who breathed this soul or mind into man, and who stamped the objective race with His image; and He alone can redeem His own, can heal the nation of its disease.

The theory that God is a principle, a boundless ocean of life, pervading all things alike, leads to a vague and hopeless state of mind in the end. To those who in early life have been greatly shocked by severe Puritanical teachings, this theory gives a sense of boundless freedom, at first extremely satisfactory, as the higher nature always rebels against the doctrine of an angry or jealous God; but in time there comes, in place of this mental exhilaration, a feeling of loss, a sense of being alone and unprotected. An individual in this state of mind is as a ship on a boundless ocean without compass, rudder or anchor.

Man in his present state of development instinctively yearns for some power greater than himself, some source of wisdom in whom he may trust, and whom he may love. The spiritual Man yearns for the father—mother—the source of his being; he does not long for the principle of a being, but for the being itself.

Christ, while with men, constantly taught of a Supreme Being, whom He named "Father." Not His Father alone, but "The Father." "I speak that which I have seen with my Father." "I came from the Father," and "I go to the Father." Christ in all of his teachings endeavored to present God in an attractive light, so that His followers would not only understand the nature of the Father, but would trust and love Him also; and not only trust and love Him, but become like Him.

We understand that at this juncture in his journey, the average man cannot comprehend the modus operandi of the creative plan, or the Creator. He has not even fathomed the law through which the simplest flower unfolds its beauty to the sun. How then can he be expected to apprehend that stupendous operation by which worlds and races of men are evolved.

But there are vital points connected with this subject which for his safety and advancement he should understand. First of all, his divine origin, his spiritual nature, his intimate relations to the Christ, his limitless mental capacity and will power, his power of creating and re-creating. He must also understand his religious nature and needs; he must know that he can become whatever he desires.

"A man is a bundle of relations, a knot of roots, whose flower and fruitage is the world. * * *. Human labor, through all its forms, from the sharpening of a stake to the construction of a city or an epic, is one immense illustration of the perfect compensation of the universe."

—Emerson.

"Man, what thou art is hidden from thyself.
Know'st not, that morning, mid-day and the eve
Are all within thee? The ninth heaven art thou;
And from the spheres into the roar of time
Did'st fall ere while. Thou art the brush that painted
The hues of all the world—the light of life,
That ranged its glory in the nothingness."

—Ferridoddin.

"We will adjourn," said Father Hyacinth at the close of the lesson, stepping from the platform and greeting in his loving way the members of the class that thronged about him.

"Children, you hear that;" pointing toward the great clock that was just then striking ten. "This is to be an important day for our little world," he continued. "There will be two or three hundred visitors, no doubt, and you have each a mission to these outside members of the great brotherhood. I want you all to try and see what kindness, patience and love will do toward making these outsiders one with us. We shall all need to exert ourselves in order to entertain them as royally as we desire to do. Come now," looking back and smiling, "we must commence work."

In a few moments the audience had dispersed, each individual obeying the call of duty or the prompting of inclination. The Boston man, who appeared inclined to be sociable with me this morning, proposed that we should unfold the chairs and arrange them about the tables, which had been opened and placed in order.

Brother Paul said that we should require all of the reserved seats in the town. This being the season of small fruits and roses, the crowd would be unusually large.

After completing our task of placing the chairs the Boston man said, "Now let's take our chairs out under that grand old tree yonder," pointing to a majestic redwood on the edge of the lawn, "and have a chat and watch the Brethren set the tables. I have travelled extensively in nearly every portion of the habitable globe in search of curiosities, sights and sounds, and, taking it all in all, I have never found a spot so full of interest, so perfect in every respect, so nearly ideal, as this. It appears to me to be a demonstration of what is best and wisest in human nature—solving the problem of man's possibilities. What do you think about it?" turning abruptly to me.

"I am not wise, neither do I know much about the world," I replied, "but the people here seem so honest, truthful and happy; everything appears very different from anything that I have ever known."

At this moment John and Annie joined us. John looking serene and comfortable, as usual; and Annie in one of her facetious and excitable moods. Coming up to me, she said, "Elizabeth, I must go home. If I stay here much longer I shall be converted, especially if Brother Paul chooses me again as his companion in inspecting the fruit orchards. I think I shall need two or three more reincarnations in order to get rid of my 'badness,' as John calls it. Don't you think so, Elizabeth?" turning toward me a face as honest and sweet as a child's.

"If there is one thing that I do desire above another," I replied, "it is that in some of your incarnations you may evolve the faculty of speaking the truth, for if there is anything I prize it is honesty and truthfulness in those who profess to love me."

"You dear soul," she cried, throwing her arms about me and beaming upon me, "you will have your heart's desire concerning me if I remain here long. They are all so awfully good you can't quarrel with anybody. You can't be bad; there's nobody to be bad with, especially since you are getting regenerated," looking me full in the eyes. "This is a curious place up here," shaking her head and looking as sober as a judge. "I have been about the world a good bit,—not so extensively as our distinguished friend here,"—nodding toward the Boston man, "but more than many, and I will say that I never saw such a place and such a people. Here are over three hundred persons, men and women thrown together up in this wilderness, hundreds of miles from civilization, some of them not having been off the place in a dozen years; and yet all, to a man and a woman, having high-bred manners, being uniformly courteous, cheerful, obliging, self-sacrificing, and the most wonderful of all speaking the English language correctly. Gracefully and artistically clothed. People that when you come in contact with them you feel that you are with ladies and gentlemen, no matter what may be their color or occupation. Society where a gentleman can smile upon a lady, or give a pleasing compliment, without being in love with her or desiring her to be in love with him."

"The unusual conditions and practices among these people are what make this little world up here in the mountains what it is," said John. "I learn that, during the fifty odd years that have passed since the little band of pilgrims first settled on this spot, there has never been a case of intoxication, an ounce of tobacco used, a quarrel, or a blow struck in anger, on the plantation. There are no lawyers or doctors on the place, neither marriages nor divorces. These facts explain to you why this unusual atmosphere pervades the whole settlement."

"That is just where the trouble is with me," cried Annie. "I can't be so good. I like a good fight now and then, and I dote on love-making, marriages and especially divorces. These things are all there is in life to me; at least, so far as I have been able to see. I tell you I am not good enough to live up here with these people," stamping her feet by way of emphasis.

"Never mind," said John, "perhaps you are better than you know. Come, we will go down to the station and welcome the visitors; they will bring you a taste of that world which you like so much." And drawing her arm within his own strong protecting one they walked off toward the station, Annie looking back and smiling like a spoiled child.

The Boston man and I sat in silence for several minutes after they had left us. At last my companion said to me, "Which of all the women who appear to adore that handsome brother of yours will he be likely to marry?"

"None of them," I replied; "he will never marry."

"And why not?" he asked with some asperity.

"Well—because he is not made that way," I answered in slangy parlance.

That polished Boston man gazed at me for some moments, his whole manner plainly denoting disgust. At length he said, "You know better than to make use of any such expressions. There is nothing 'smart,' as you call it, in their use; on the contrary, it is incorrect and inelegant."

"I know that," I replied. "It is another proof of the science of that automatic action of the brain that we hear so much of in these days."

"More properly speaking, the automatic action of the tongue; the brain had little to do with the matter, the tongue talked itself," said the Bostonian sourly.

We sat for some moments in silence. I knew that my companion was correct and that I had shown an unattractive side, but I had the Yankee element known as "spunk" strong in me with a desire for the last word, so I strengthened my spinal column and said, "I should judge that a large proportion of the conversation in general society was automatic; from the tongue only. Place a group of garrulous people together, start them off on some subject, and it talks itself. There would not be expressed one thought in hours of such talk. We are very sure to stop talking as soon as we begin to think. The 'thinkers' of the world have not been talkers."

"Your logic is better than your language, Sister," my companion said with mock gravity, and rising he offered me his arm, and with a courtly air said, "Will you permit me to escort you to dinner, which has just been announced?"

"Yes," I answered, "you no doubt consider

by this time that I am in need of a tutor or guardian."

"Well, yes; I discovered there are a few things for you to learn yet," looking at me with that high and mighty air which some men assume while looking at a woman whom they consider as their inferior.

"I was not aware that any of us up here could lay claim to a knowledge of all things," I returned spitefully, as we took our seats at the table. I did not look at my companion for some time, but could feel that he literally shook with suppressed laughter; over what I have no idea.

The excursion party was on time, and unusually large, one of the most successful that had yet been given. The air of kindliness and genuine politeness exhibited by the members of the community toward the visitors made a most favorable impression. A close inspection was made into the various branches of industry on the plantation, and their original and improved methods greatly astonished the leading business men, who had come largely out of curiosity. All were evidently surprised at the elegance and perfect finish of the buildings, particularly that of the Home.

Brother Paul said that these excursions were

of great value to the Institution, making it better understood, and adding to its strength in every way. He said that three families had on this occasion planned with Father Hyacinth to enter the Home this season on probation. Also that this had been one of the most remunerative expeditions they had yet known, requiring an extra car to ship the supplies from the Home to the junction. The visitors appeared inclined to purchase everything they saw in the line of food, the quality being so superior and the prices reasonable beyond any thing they had ever known. Sister Irene, who superintends the apiary, reported the sale of three hundred and fifty pounds of honey.

April 15th, 7 p. m.

Order and comparative silence have been again restored to this blessed retreat. Brother Rameses has been for the past hour giving in his inimitable style on the violin the plaintive airs of his native land, until the spirit of Peace has spread her wings over all, causing one to feel like blessing rather than condemning. In my heart I forgave that Boston man for his evident belief in his own superiority over women, and as

I thought it all over I repeated to myself in my favorite slang, "He is not to blame, he is made that way."

10 p. m.

The chimes have just sounded the hour for retiring, and silence broods over all that was so recently the scene of animation and life.

Annie declared as she was dropping off to sleep that this had been the eventful day of her whole life. Why or how she did not inform me.

CHAPTER III.

Benares, California, April 24th.

It was announced at the breakfast table that Sister Alicia would give the morning lesson in place of Father Hyacinth, who had been called away, and the subject is to be the Fall of Man. I hope she will not let him down too hard, for I don't believe that all of the men fell.

Annie and I, while waiting for the bell to sound for the class, were out on the lawn walking up and down enjoying the mountain air laden with the fragrance of the trees and flowers that crowded each other up the mountain side.

Annie took out her pencil and sharpened it most carefully, and unrolled her note paper, saying, "I want to take down every word of the lesson this morning," smoothing out her paper. "Our old minister told me, when I went to him for information, not to ask too many questions, that I was too young to understand such subjects."

"Would you have been any better off if you had known?" I asked.

"Why of course I would; wouldn't I?" she asked in astonishment. "What are we all up here listening to these lessons for if they are no good?"

"Such things are all right for us to know, I suppose, if by knowing them we live better lives and are kinder to those about us," I replied.

"Well, that will do," she said, pulling me along toward the Home. "We get preaching enough in the chapels without your prattle. But I am getting more interested in the lessons every day, though they were awfully poky at first. Brother Paul has explained many things to me. He is too nice for anything. I think it is just ridiculous that these Brothers up here can't marry!"—jerking out her words with a vengeance.

"Do they desire to do so?" I asked, in astonishment.

"Well, no; not that I know of," she answered slowly. "I suppose that John will be more queer and outlandish than ever when he gets back home, won't he?"

"I think John will join this brotherhood," I answered, after a moment's pause.

"Well I guess not!" Throwing back her head, her black eyes fairly blazing. "You don't suppose for a moment that he would leave you for any brotherhood, do you?"

"But I should come up here too," I said, looking seriously at her.

"Not if I can prevent it, you may be sure," she said sniffing the air and tossing her head defiantly.

"Annie," I said, drawing her arm through mine, and taking her hand in a firm clasp, "I have come to the conclusion that John takes the correct view of life, and I know that he tries to live up to what he considers to be right, just and loyal toward all men. And I, like King Agrippa, am almost pursuaded to be a Christian. Loving you as I do, I have hoped that you would view life in a different way from what we have always seen it. That is, more earnest and helpful to those in trouble—yes, and more kindly. Loving people more, and seeing fewer faults in them."

She did not raise her head, or speak for several minutes; at last she said, tears filling her eyes, "My dear, I am not nearly so bad as I appear on the surface; I think of many things of which I never speak. My early life as a newspaper reporter developed in me a disposition to levity. I was nothing, unless I was funny. My occupation had a tendency to smother in me everything that was earnest and true. I had the reputation of being one of the wittiest writers of the day; I grew into the habit of turning everything into ridicule; nothing escaped me. I sacrificed my best friends to my wit. The habit has grown upon me, until people appear ridiculous to me. But I am not so severe and critical as I used to be; I have more patience with what I call people's idiosyncrasies, and know that I have grown kindlier toward the human race since I came up here. So don't be disheartened, dear," putting her arms about me and caressing me in her inimitable manner, "I may be converted yet, though I may try your patience in many ways. This false way of viewing things has become second nature to me, and I shall transgress before I am aware of it. I am a demonstration of your theory of the automatic action of the tongue— it will talk itself."

The great bell just now pealed out the hour for service and cut short our conversation. We entered the chapel in time to listen to the music and hear the reading of the lesson, which was from the seventeenth chapter of St. John's gospel.

I observed that the Boston man had a seat on the other side of John, and was looking unusually modest and humble, an attitude I considered decidedly becoming to him.

When Sister Alicia stepped forward and stood in silence for a few seconds, I could not take my eyes from her beautiful face; such a feeling of pride arose in my heart that she was a woman, and that I was a woman—I like men awfully well, but there is something about a woman that I like more than awfully well—but when she began to talk I forgot all about her being a woman or anything else. All I could do was just to listen, and I think Annie never took her eyes from her. It was so soothing to notice the graceful fall of her Greek costume as she would make appropriate gestures from time to time. Women are more beautiful than men, there is no denying the fact.

"Look how the floor of heaven
　Is thick inlaid with patines of bright gold:
　There's not the smallest orb which thou behold'st
　But in his motion like an angel sings,
　Still quiring to the young-eyed cherubims;
　Such harmony is in immortal souls;
　But whilst this muddy vesture of decay
　Doth grossly close it in, we cannot hear it."

　　　　　　　　　　—Merchant of Venice.

THIRD LESSON.

MAN'S MISTAKE.

From our Scriptures and all other sacred histories we learn that the human family, somewhere in remote ages, transgressed a divine law, out of which has grown all of the suffering of the world—disease, decay and death. Ancient prophets and seers declare that man brought all forms of suffering upon himself through his disobedience of a law controlling his physical being.

There have been a few adepts in occult science who have stated what that sin was and what law was broken, but these statements have never been placed in a familiar light before the student of sacred history, so there is a general misunderstanding as to the what or how or when of the catastrophe. But all believers in our Bible, Christian or otherwise, hold steadfastly to the belief that our forefathers, at some period of the journey of life, deliberately took matters into their own hands which brought about the present condition of things, but no one appears willing to tell just what that sin was.

Mankind must have done something.

According to our Scriptures, the race was given control over the earth in all of its glory, "And out of the ground made the Lord God to grow every tree that is pleasant to the sight, and good for food; and the tree of life also in the midst of the garden, and the tree of knowledge of good and evil. And the Lord God said to this people, Of every tree of the garden thou mayest freely eat; but of the tree of the knowledge of good and evil, thou shalt not eat of it: for in the day that thou eatest thereof thou shalt surely die."

We understand that this did not relate to the death of the body alone, as we know death, but to the degeneracy of the soul; to the introduction of disease, decay and death into every kingdom upon the earth.

One of the undisputed privileges of all divinely created beings is FREE Will, with the right to use it; which the Divine Power cannot deny.

There came a phase in the growth of the race when there was developed an insatiable hunger to know more concerning the working of the divine law of life. Not alone were these children of the Divine given the use of Free Will, but they were also given the privilege of solving all apparent hidden mysteries. These angelic beings were informed that if they would know all things, they must come in touch with all things, and suffer all things. They, nothing daunted, said, "Father, give us the portion that falleth to us." And this family of the Infinite "took its journey into a far country, and THERE WASTED ITS SUBSTANCE IN RIOTOUS LIVING."

I wish to make some statements here that I fear may shock some, because of the strangeness and newness of the thought; but we must bear in mind that there is nothing new.

Now the original God-created race was androgynous, or hermaphroditic, when it started out on that journey. The divine plan of populating the world at that time was through immaculate conception. In those later and degenerate days, Mary, the mother of our Lord, came as a perfect and normal type of the original race that inhabited our globe before sin came. Christ following, revealing in perfection the divine dual man, and coming in the original order of reproduction; not the result of a miracle.

In the third era, we learn that man was formed of the dust of the ground, and that the Lord God "breathed into his nostrils the breath of life; and he became a living soul." Here is a decided change from the first race which was in the divine image. Something had been added thereto. To "become" is to pass from one state or condition into another. Doubtless in that garden of the Lord, where He walked "in the cool of the day," there passed cycles of time, during which Man was still an angelic being, although he had come into possession of a form to suit his needs.

Then again another countless sweep of time—ages, too vast to comprehend—and we hear,

"And the Lord God caused a deep sleep to fall upon Adam—or Man—and he slept." That "deep sleep" that fell upon the race was a clouding of the spiritual understanding and an awakening into material consciousness. At this stage we hear not only of man, but also of woman, and we learn that they have bodies of flesh. "Unto Adam also and unto his wife did the Lord God make coats of skins, and clothed them."

The few thousand years generally accepted as the age of the planet and the race is not so much as the dawn of one of the creative periods known as the six days of creation. Time is among man's inventions. In the divine ordering there is no Time. "One day is with the Lord as a thousand years; and a thousand years is as one day."

During the figurative "sleep" which fell upon

mankind, great changes were wrought in mind, body and environments. Marked differences occurred in the bodily formations; there was produced what scientists have named as differentiation of the sex: the evolution of individual man and individual woman, in place of those dual beings, those "Sons of God," who in the beginning peopled our planet.

What has always been known as the "Fall of Man" was the gradual descent of the celestial Man into what we call animal generation, the production of animal man; the race having fallen into an abnormal state of mind, in time manifested a marked change in bodily form, a change that rendered the propagation of the animal man possible, an artificial method of reproducing the race.

This was that great sin which Man was forbidden to commit; it was that fruit of the tree of knowledge which he was commanded not to touch, unless he was willing to take the penalty, which was death and everything that goes to bring it.

It required countless periods of time to develop those physical malformations necessary to render animal generation among men possible. In all probability but a small portion came under this curse at the beginning. We read: "And it came to pass, when man began to multiply on the face of the earth, and daughters were born to them, that the Sons of God saw the daughters of men that they were fair, and they took them wives of all which they chose * * * and they bore children to them."

Those "Sons of God" were of the celestial family who had not yet lost their original conformation. The daughters of men were of the fleshly generation. From those "Sons of God" and "daughters of men" came our present race.*

According to all geological survey, the recovery of the Mastodons and other monstrous shapes, showing the slow stages of development, there must have been incalculably long reaches of time, countless ages, during which shifting periods nothing but confusion, discord and suffering existed upon the sorrowful planet. A period of darkness, before the full establishment of the law of human propagation; a reign of terror; such hideous forms, such monstrosities as were produced through that man-made law can

---

* There are many evidences of man's dual nature still extant—certain physical conformations that have always aroused much discussion, especially among the more earnest students of anatomy. The human body is a dual structure both in form and function. Physiologists have never done with questioning why the brain was in pairs, and why the nerves travel in pairs from the medulla to the feet. Then, too, careful students have long questioned the purpose of the rudimentary mammary glands in the male species; evidently they were not intended for ornament, as what we call Nature, creates only for use. Anyone familiar with the study of anatomy must be impressed with the similarity between the male and female organizations, especially in the organs of generation.

scarcely be comprehended by the human mind. We read, "There were giants in the earth in those days."

All of the lower kingdoms upon the earth suffered alike from the sin. Through man's sex-transgression there was engendered a deadly virus, becoming a race contagion, and being by degrees infused into the life of all the lower kingdoms.

From our sacred authority we read: "The Lord said unto Adam, Because thou hast hearkened unto the voice of thy wife, and hast eaten of the tree, of which I commanded thee, saying, Thou shalt not eat of it; cursed is the ground for thy sake; in sorrow shalt thou eat of it all the days of thy life; thorns and thistles shall it bring forth to thee. In the sweat of thy face shalt thou eat bread. And God saw that the wickedness of man was great in the earth, and that every imagination of the thoughts of his heart was evil continually, * * * for the earth was filled with violence, * * * for all flesh has corrupted his way upon the earth. * * * And the Lord said, My spirit shall not always strive with man, for that he also is flesh."

Man here referred to was doubtless those remnants of the androgynous race fast becoming extinct through physical union with the "daughters of men." "And the Lord God said, Behold the man (the race) has become as one of us, to know good and evil; and now, lest he put forth his hand, and take also of the tree of life, and eat, and live forever; therefore the Lord God sent him forth from the garden of Eden. * * He drove out the man. And he placed at the east of the garden of Eden Cherubims, and a flaming sword which turned every way, to keep the way of the tree of life."

The race having disobeyed the divine command, and transgressed a spiritual law, or rather having substituted the law of flesh for the law of spirit, had become as creators; had through the eating of that "tree of knowledge of good and evil" brought forth the man of flesh, in which exists all evil. In order that this self-created race should not lay hold of and eat the tree of life and live forever in its transgressions and crimes, hosts of cherubims, spirits of fire with their flaming swords of death, were placed at the entrance of the eternal life. Thus we see that through the sins of fleshly man alone death entered into the world.

The chief point of importance in this lesson is the fact that the divine Man, the true Man, being created androgynous, cannot be changed any more than God can be changed. Each individual is dual in the spiritual nature; each is a union of the divine feminine and divine masculine still. The apparent division is in the external shell, the body only, and that is the creation wholly of the fleshly or carnal mind, in which, as we have seen, exists all wrongs.

The race belief in the division of the sex has had the tendency to accentuate the leading characteristics of both man and woman; developing in the male character a disposition to be severe, harsh, dictatorial and tyrannical, because deprived of the softening influence of the womanly nature, being as a kingdom divided against itself.

Man believes himself to be a single, separate individual, having a feminine counterpart somewhere in the universe wandering up and down in search of him. While the woman is unceasingly seeking for her "twin soul," both as wretched as human beings can be, for they always make the mistake and take their neighbor's "counterpart" or "twin soul."

Paracelsus said, centuries ago, "There is perhaps no doctrine which has done more mischief than the misconstrued teaching about 'soul affinities' and 'soul marriages,' because such a doctrine is willingly accepted by the carnal mind. God did not create souls in halves; nor can

Adam find his Eve again, unless she grow within his heart."

The masculine characteristics displayed in the strongest specimens of manhood are great courage, strength of purpose, love of self, steadfastness, truthfulness, bravery, with the power to reason, analyze and especially to command. These are considered to be exclusively the characteristics of man. While the set of faculties considered as purely feminine are love of home and offspring, tenderness, patience, faithfulness, mercy, and intuition, with the desire for self-sacrifice. These qualities of course render her so much more docile, gentle and easily commanded by the thoroughly masculine man.

Bayard Taylor says, "Genius is always hermaphroditic, adding the male element to the woman and the female to the man."

Those self-poised, commanding, useful, and independent women, who have been foremost in all works for the emancipation and elevation of humanity, have developed the dual mind and nature. They have manifested strength of purpose, courage, sense of justice, truthfulness, with the power to reason, analyze and command, blended with all of the sweet and gentle feminine traits.

Such women have not considered it sufficient

that men should monopolize and use those elements of strength alone. They have developed these so-called masculine qualities in themselves, and yet have lost nothing of their feminine grace and sweetness. Indeed they have been the more merciful, more loving, more self-sacrificing for the uniting of the two natures.

The noblest of men have possessed in their characters a blending of love with justice, devotion with courage, patience with strength; and with their power to reason, analyze and command, the woman's intuition and desire for self-sacrifice.

Each to a degree have returned to the androgynous type. There have been, and there are still, many such who stand out in sublime relief above the race. Such have been the tenderest, strongest, most faithful and patient of men; the wisest, kindest, grandest and most helpful of women.

All such have entered into that "kingdom of God" where they shall no longer be "twain" but "one flesh."

This state or condition is the marriage of the divine love and wisdom, the feminine and masculine natures in the individual.

The teaching and demonstrating of this vital truth was one of the most important of Christ's mission. The recovery of that nature in man was that "kingdom of God" concerning the nature of which He so emphasized in all of His lessons. "Neither shall they say, Lo, here! or lo, there! for, behold, the kingdom of God is within you."

Christ was a perfect example of the celestial marriage—the dual individual—and was therefore called the "Bridegroom." John the Baptist said of Him: "The Bridegroom is He who possesses the bride. He must increase; I must decrease."

While Christ, in speaking of John, said: "I say unto you, Among those born of woman, there is not a greater than John, yet the least in the kingdom of God is superior to him." Because John had not attained to that celestial union—the two-in-one—or had not become conscious of it.

Jacob Boehme says:

"What is mystically called the end of the world is the end of external or physical generation, and will be when the man has again found the woman within himself; from whom he has become separated by his descending from his spiritual state and becoming gross and material. The man is not without the woman. That is to say, the paradisiacal man is still male and female in one. But man having ceased to be lord, and become servant to the animal kingdom in him, has ceased to recognize the true woman within, his heavenly bride, and seeks for the woman in that which is external to him. Therefore man cannot enter into his original state of unity and purity except by means of the celestial marriage in his own soul."

To the weak and oppressed feminine portion of the race life has always presented a serious aspect. Woman has always been a prey to evil influences because of her historical weakness. The literal interpretation of the story concerning the formation of Eve, that rib business and its incorporation into all religions and creeds, has caused a deep and lasting prejudice against womankind wherever the story has been told. It is a race hypnotization.

According to the received authority, the Lord instructed Adam as to what he should and should not do, while Eve was left to herself to be tempted, to bring disaster not alone to the human family, but a curse to all of the lower kingdoms and the planet itself.

The universal belief is that the weight of the whole calamity of the Fall of Man rests wholly upon the woman. This has been the teaching, so that it is not strange that she should be under the bondage of that belief. Woman's natural inferiority and wickedness has become a race belief, so that notwithstanding all of her efforts to elevate herself, she still maintains a humiliated position, from which man in his present state is not likely to help to elevate her.

This false teaching has influenced and biased the judgment of many of our most gifted and grand men. Paul, that wise and enlightened mystic, has left through his teaching a spirit of bondage for the women of all Christendom.

It is one of the marked characteristics of the mind of flesh to degrade the woman. So true is this of the carnal mind, that the average women, as a rule, do not love, cherish and sympathize with each other. It is only those advanced, cultured and broadly humane of the sisterhood that love all womenkind and who labor for their advancement and upbuilding. Such unconsciously recognize the divine woman in all. And it will be only when the man becomes conscious of the divine woman within himself that women, as a race, will receive a just recognition.

The mystery of the divine feminine is the central truth in the Catholic religion, and explains their worship of the "Mother."

One of the fatal results of the fall of the race

into animal generation was the reincarnation of the soul into new bodies on this planet. Through sin man entered upon the ever-circling wheel of Time, where he will revolve and continue to revolve in the narrow circuit of death, and re-birth, until his regeneration or the resurrection of his divine mate within.

The soul had its mission to perform on this plane of existence, but having come under the control of the carnal mind—the mind of the flesh—it lost sight of the errand upon which it was sent, and has therefore become "earthbound;" and according to the carnal law, the law controlling the earth under man, it will be compelled to re-embody until it either learns that for which it was created, or passes out of being, and becomes as chaff from the "mills of God."

Milton pictures this state or condition of the soul:

"But when lust
By unchaste looks, loose gestures, and foul talk,
But most by lewd and lavish acts of sin,
Lets in defilement to the inward parts,
The soul grows clotted by contagion,
Imbodies, and imbrutes, till she quite lose
The divine property of her first being."

Re-embodiment is the law governing all physical life; and reincarnation of the race into new bodies and new environments is but the fulfillment of that law. Man takes upon himself many guises, according to the status of his mind and desires, and his progress toward the object of his creation, or his dissolution.

There are many grades in the school which he has entered, and he will be environed to suit his grade. Where he may be placed, on what planet, with what surroundings during his later term of schooling, is not for him to know just now. The eternal law of fitness will govern all. One who holds in tenderest love the least and lowliest among us has promised that there shall be a place for all. "In my Father's house there are many mansions; if it were not so, I would have told you. I go to prepare a place for you, * * . * that where I am there ye may be also."

The religious teaching that man came into existence for the first time here upon this planet, on which he lives a brief span, sins, suffers and dies, and goes into a changeless state of bliss or woe, or out entirely, according to his merits or nature, is, as a body of teaching, most unsatisfactory and crippling to the mind; because there is in man an impulse toward progress and spiritual enlightenment. It is the promptings of the divine life within him. It was that impulse that forced him out on his tour of inspection and investigation. All teachings that limit his mental and spiritual powers cause him to retrograde. This is the condition in which we find mankind at the present time.

We have been taught that inasmuch as man has degraded himself, he must likewise elevate himself. Even a Christ or God has not the power to save a soul that WILL NOT rise above the carnal life.

All knowledge upon these subjects will be of no real value to mankind so long as the mind of the world rules.

That old and hackneyed story of being "born again" is not mere cant, as many of you believe, but has in it a vital truth. It simply signifies that the individual has laid aside his carnal mind, and come into possession of his divine Mind, which consists of all understanding just as fast as he unfolds it. It is like laying aside a worn and filthy garment, and assuming a new one of rich and lasting fabric, fashioned in a pleasing and graceful style. He has met with a change of mind instead of heart, as we were wont to call it, and as his higher Mind gradually unfolds he will grow to lay less stress on this life, so short and unsatisfactory, which is but a little term in that existence of ever-increasing knowledge and understanding, of which this life is but an hour's schooling.

"The object of man's existence is to be a Man, including all that this term implies. To re-establish the harmony which originally existed between him and the divine state, before the separation took place which disturbed the equilibrium. * * * To re-establish this harmony, man may bring the will of God to perfect expression in his nature by learning to know within himself the will of God, and being obedient to it, and thereby his own nature, and finally even the whole of the Macrocosm, may become spiritualized and be rendered paradisiacal.

—Paracelsus.

CHAPTER IV.

Benares, California, May 4th.

This morning, before the hour for our lesson, Annie and myself started out on an exploring expedition up the mountain side in quite a new direction. Following a well-traveled roadway we came suddenly upon a strange looking building, quite out of sight of the Home buildings, built in the side of the mountain, and of large blocks of the native stone, giving it an appearance of great solidity. At the one entrance was a massive iron door, and I noticed it had one large chimney. There were no other buildings near.

"This must be where they store their dynamite," I said, after studying the strange structure for a time.

"Dynamite!" exclaimed Annie. "What possible use could they have for such an explosive material away up here, out of the world?"

"For blasting rocks," I suggested.

"Oh, but these people don't do any such rackety things up here," she persisted. "They don't believe in doing anything that disturbs their equilibrium; that breaks the serene harmony of their environments. They don't want to have their atoms jarred or shocked—so that stately individual called Rameses informed me."

I was disgusted with the girl's flippancy and utter lack of seriousness; I turned and studied her for a moment, she returning my gaze innocently and patiently.

"You incorrigible little heathen! I wonder if you really have a soul?" I asked, looking at her in amazement.

"I don't think I have," she replied soberly. "I think that my other half has never been evolved yet, and Brother Paul says that we do not have a soul till that takes place."

I looked at her in silence. I know that she did not believe one word of what she had been saying; and yet her countenance was as serene and unruffled and as innocent as a babe's. For the first time in all of my acquaintance with this girl a feeling of impatience toward her seized me.

"I do wish that you could be honest and sincere occasionally," I blurted out, and turned from her and walked away.

At this moment two of the Brothers came around the base of the mountain and joined us, and I asked them the purpose of the odd-looking building.

"It is our crematory," one of them replied. "Here are cremated all animal remains."

"What do you do with your animals when they become disabled, or too old for further use? You never make any use of animal food, and I am told that you never sell a live creature from the place," questioned Annie.

"In the first place, we take the best possible care of our animals," said the younger of the two men, "and by that means they live and remain active to a much greater age than do domestic animals generally. As soon as they become too old for use, or disabled in any manner, we turn them out in a large inclosure prepared for the purpose, which we call our hospital. In this there are comfortable stables and plenty of fresh and delicious water. Our animals that have become superannuated or disabled are cared for as carefully as when in their prime."

"We love our animals," said the elder of the two men, his face glowing with enthusiasm, "and we care for them as tenderly as we would the human members of our family. When they become utterly helpless our surgeon applies a little chloroform, and in a few moments they are at rest, without a struggle; then the remains are cremated and that ends the matter."

"Matters are quite different with us in regard to such things," remarked Annie. "When our domestic animals get too old for service, our cows are sent away to be converted into steaks and roasts, and our dear old pet horses into bologna sausage and canned beef."

The two brethren smiled at Annie's sarcasm, and asked us if we enjoyed that sort of diet.

Just here the great bell sounded the quarter to nine, and we all descended together, reaching the chapel in time to hear the chanting and sit through their five minutes' heavenly silence.

The subject for this morning's lesson is of unusual interest to me; anything of an occult nature at once arouses my curiosity. Much in the teachings here explains to me John's peculiar views and mode of life. Each day since I came here I have learned a lesson, each one showing me how little I really knew that was of any importance in life.

There appeared to be an air pervading the chapel this morning unlike anything that I had ever experienced in any other room or building; and as I sat, with closed eyes, listening to the tremulous tones of the organ and the low sweet voices chanting the psalms, I experienced a strange thrill throughout my entire being; many new and strange thoughts came to me; and I recalled that command that was given to the chosen few, to remain in Jerusalem until they were baptized with the Holy Spirit; and I questioned as to the nature of that Holy Spirit. I also recalled the fact that that Presence and that promise of Power was not given to the apostles of that time and that place alone, but to the devoted lovers and followers at all times and in all places made sacred to Him. And my heart opened up to the world, and I embraced all in love, and I forgave Annie and clasped her hand in mine.

Father Hyacinth stood for some moments motionless after the singing ceased. These periods of silence appeared more impressive to me than words however eloquent, but I was scarcely prepared for the lesson of the morning; indeed it opened into an entirely new and strange world, but one which commends itself nevertheless to my inner consciousness.

FOURTH LESSON.

NATURE SPIRITS.

Man has developed the sense-life on the animal plane to such a degree that it is impossible for him to comprehend those silent and subtle forces that move the universe. For instance, fire and electricity, two elements of common everyday use, yet wholly unknown to him as naked forces. He can only see and feel the workings of those hidden laws.

It is the same with the Elemental world; a world of semi-intellectual beings which largely control the elements—the earth, water, fire and air—the human race is at all times more or less under the influence of these beings, without knowing how to defend themselves against their assaults. Man should know how to control these beings as well as he now does light, air, water and electricity. He now moulds many things to his use that he does not know the basic principles of at all.

From all occult writings we ascertain that there have been large numbers of men—and women also—who have been perfectly familiar with those denizens of the invisible universe. Not only been cognizant of them, but able to control them.

These were the demons and devils spoken of by Christ, and which his disciples commanded and controlled. The Vedantic authorities call this class of life Elementals; in our Bible they are spoken of as cherubims and angels.

Zechariah, in describing one of his visions, says: "Then I said unto the angel who talked with me, What are these, my lord? And the angel answered and said unto me, These are the four spirits of the heavens, which go forth from standing before the Lord of all the earth."

Ezekiel's visions appeared to be of the same nature, he said: "Also out of the midst thereof came the likeness of four living creatures. And this was their appearance; they had the likeness of a man * * * * and I knew that they were cherubims. And the cherubims lifted up their wings from the earth in my sight."

We consider our Scriptures to be the most reliable authority on occult matters, and they are full of proofs of the existence of these Nature Spirits. They also teach of other classes of spirits, some of which are of the most diabolical type, and do not belong to the elements, but are such as entered into the swine during the ministry of Christ.

There is a deeply occult lesson in that story of the devils entering into the swine, which would be most profitable for the new class to study carefully. I cannot in this connection explain, because it would open a vast field of study and speculation too wide and deep for the occasion.

Cornelius Agrippa says: "As the spirits of darkness be stronger in the dark, so good spirits, which be angels of light, are augmented not only by the divine light of the sun, but also by our common wood fires; and as the celestial fire drives away dark spirits, so also this our fire of wood doth the same."

Here the question will naturally arise, Are these the spirits of departed human beings?

No; we are not dealing with the spirits of the so-called dead, but with a world of life, with its thousands of different forms over which we are to obtain control. Man, if he did but know it, is superior to these subordinate kingdoms. "I have said, Ye are Gods!" declared David.

No; those Spirits of which we have been talking are the Elementals of the Vedas, and the cherubims and seraphims of our Bible. Certain species of the Elementals are those spirits of darkness alluded to in the occult philosophies. The angels of light being the seraphims, a very high order of intelligence, that have a most important mission to mankind for good.

Our inability to see the inhabitants of the spiritual world does not thereby separate us from them, all of which are powerful factors for good or ill to the race and the planet.

Man's descent into animal generation was the commencement of a species of hostility to be waged against him by the unseen. He had transgressed a divinely established law by which the rights of those hosts in the unseen region had been usurped.

"Evil spirits are, so to say, bailiffs and executioners of God. They have been called into existence by the influence of evil, and they work out their destiny," declares Paracelsus.

In the divine plan, man had a mission to these beings, as all higher types have to the lower; but he, forgetting his divine origin, and going into business on his own responsibility on the animal plane, aroused a deadly antagonism in the Elemental worlds, which had been, during his state of innocence, a great strength and power for good.

The truth is, they reflect all moods and states of mind. While man was pure and good, they were good. They respond to man's moods. They manifest love where love prevails, and hatred and rage where such passions predominate. All discord, from whatever cause; all bloodshed, whether from the slaughtering of men or animals; has the power to arouse the anger and excitement of these unseen hosts. In retaliation they cause the various upheavals in nature. Whenever there are any great outbreaks of human passion, they gather in great armies and join in the battle.

The fearful shock which our planet experienced during the crucifixion of our Lord was caused by the rage of those celestial armies. The fearful earthquake, the tempests and thick blackness that enveloped the land and covered Jerusalem as with a pall, rending her temple, tearing asunder her grand edifices and walls, were the work of those enraged hosts.

They make war where the spirit of war exists. They reflect the states of mind of the individual or of bodies of individuals. They reflect the strongest influence for the time. Not being reasoning creatures they act only from impulse.

According to the teaching of Paracelsus these beings have their hates and their loves. He says: "The Elementals have an aversion to self-conceited and opinionated persons, drunkards and gluttons, and to vulgar and quarrelsome people of all kinds; but they love natural men, who are simple minded and childlike, innocent and sincere."

Under pure, good and healthy influences these Spirits become powerful allies in good works. They come to the aid of the Christian healer, especially where material—so-called—environments need to be removed, changed or done away with. They are God's workers and warriors on the unseen plane.

The centurion understood this philosophy when he besought Christ to heal his servant. "I am coming and will cure him," the Master said. But the Roman said. "I am not worthy that Thou shouldest come under my roof; but only command by word, and my servant will be cured. For even I am a man, appointed under authority, having soldiers under me; I say to this one, Go, and he goes; to another, Come, and he comes; and to my servant, Do this, and he does it." Jesus said, "Be it done to thee as thou hast believed." And the servant was immediately restored. And Christ was astonished at the understanding of this hidden force manifested by an ordinary soldier.

This power was understood by the Greeks, and no doubt by the Romans largely.

Christ knew that the slightest resistance aroused the antagonism of the large bodies that follow the human family constantly; therefore non-resistance was one of the strongest points in His teaching. His was the law of love; and love cannot resist. We all know the law! "I say unto you, oppose not the injurious person; but if any one strike thee on thy right cheek, turn to him also the left."

All states of mind are contagious; the individual who indulges in the spirit of combativeness and resistance, however silently, will arouse the same low element in those about him. Not only will he arouse it in the human, but also in those hosts of Elementals that constantly surround him, and are interested in all that he thinks or does.

"Are they not all ministering spirits, sent forth to minister to them who shall be heirs of salvation?" Paul asks.

It was this mighty unseen force to which Christ referred on that night of agony and desertion in Gethsemane: "Dost thou think that I cannot intreat my Father, and He will send to my relief more than twelve legions of angels?"

The most prominent of all scriptural teaching is that of angelic and spiritual ministry; and no careful student and thorough believer in the

New Testament can have the slightest doubt of the statements concerning these powers. The seventy, on their return from their mission of healing and teaching, declared with joy: "Lord, even the demons are subject unto us by thy name." The name of Christ was as an element of peace to those fiercely disturbed armies of spiritual soldiery. "For He is our peace, having removed the enmity," Paul tells us.

Where the evil thoughts of large bodies of people are commingled, as in warfare, or political strife, where fierce animosity prevails, these Nature Spirits become so enraged, and so numerous are they, that their action upon the elements is often of the most disastrous nature, producing terrible storms, great conflagrations in towns and cities, also those destructive forest fires which are so mysterious and impossible to control.

All antagonism and resistance has the tendency to inflame and enrage these unreasoning entities. This explains Christ's spirit of non-resistance. "When he was buffeted He buffeted not back again."

As a rule they follow the strongest lead. There have been times when vast hordes of these creatures have come under the control of wicked leaders of high intelligence, who have made use of this power for evil purposes, and through which great cataclysms have occurred at various periods of the world's history.

Paul, who understood the nature and influence of these denizens of the unseen world, not only upon the elements, but upon the human and animal creation, tried to forcibly impress upon his students the fact of the constant warfare between the carnal mind and these unseen armies. He says, "Stand fast therefore in the liberty wherewith Christ has made you free, and be not entangled again in the yoke of bondage, wherein in times past you all walked according to the course of this world, according to the prince of the power of the air, the spirit that now worketh in the children of disobedience."

Another occult writer says: "There are good Spirits and Spirits of evil; planetary Spirits and angels. There are the Spirits of the four elements, and there are many thuosands of different kinds. Men have their leaders and authorities; bees and ants their queens; and all animals have their leaders. So also have the Spirits of nature their kings and queens." *

Mankind must come into the knowledge of the Elemental world in order to control and command this power as they now do fire, elec-

---

* Paracelsus.

tricity and other unseen forces. It will be impossible for the race to become regenerated without a certain knowledge of these kingdoms.

For illustration, take the elements of fire and water, both indispensable to the maintenance of all life; and yet how destructive to life when not under the control of man. A child is early taught this much of science, that he may avoid danger. Christ, during his ministry, made known the existence of these beings to his apostles, and also instructed them as to the law by which the Elemental life was controlled.

While none of us understand perfectly the real nature of the air which we breathe, we know that we cannot exist many seconds if it be shut away from our lungs; we therefore control this element. We know that if any foreign element be introduced into it that our lives are endangered; we understand enough of the nature of this life principle to correct all these things. It is only a step higher to the control of that Elemental life that surrounds us all, very much as the air does; we each have our "familiars," let us try and make good use of them.

As we investigate the character of these occult forces, and appreciate our absolute oneness with them all, we will not need to question why there is never a loud, harsh or angry word uttered on this plantation; and why an animal never receives a blow or an unkind word, why nothing that has life is ever tortured or slaughtered.

We esteem it a crime to entertain an angry or unkind thought, or to speak an ill word to or of another; a crime for which we shall receive due punishment; there will be no escape.

You now understand why love is the ruling principle here.

Every Brother and Sister, through a knowledge of these hidden laws, has become a master or mistress over those agents of the Most High, controlling them for wise purposes.

This spot is to be our Mount Zion. From this spot are constantly going out in all directions messages of peace and love that shall help to heal the diseased soul of our planet. On this consecrated spot is set up those ladders of light which Jacob saw in his vision; and on those ladders shall come and go those helpers of God which are promised to the children of earth.

You must all, by this time, appreciate the regenerating influence of such a nucleus as this upon that great sea of warring, brutal passions that cover the earth as the waters cover the mighty deep. You cannot fail to realize the healing and soothing influence of the united mental power of this body of earnest men and women, all united as one in the thought of love and good will toward all men.

No one can ever step upon this plantation without being benefited, or as in most instances wholly healed.

We all know that Thoughts are Things, and that to think in the line of good—to think God's thoughts—steadily, unwaveringly and hopefully, is to make tangible those thoughts. This, that we call thinking, has always been, and still is, by the majority of people called prayer.

"There are good spirits and spirits of evil; planetary spirits and angels. There are the spirits of the four elements, and there are many thousand different kinds.

"A person without any self-knowledge or self-control is made to act according to the will of these creatures; but the true philosopher acts according to the will of the Supreme, the Creator, in him.

"The four classes of nature spirits do not mix with each other. * * * They live in the four elements. * * * The Elementals have no higher principles. They are therefore not immortal. *' * * They have only animal intellects, and are incapable of spiritual development.

"As far as the personalities of the Elementals are concerned, it may be said that those belonging to the element of water resemble human beings. * * * Those of the air are greater and stronger. * * * The spirits of fire—the salamanders—are long and lean. * * * The pigmies are the spirits of the earth and are of the length of about two spans."

—Paracelsus.

This morning, at the close of the lesson, as the students dispersed, going their several ways, Annie joined me, slipping her arm through mine in a confidential manner whispered, "Now I know why I never could have that San Francisco woman come near me; I always feel when near her as if I am being rubbed down with sandpaper—or rubbed up, I don't know which. Then she dresses so horridly. I told Sister Alicia to seat her next to you, because you don't know enough to notice people's disagreeable looks and rasping auras."

"Oh! don't I; I am greatly obliged to you for your good opinion," I snapped out. "It is barely possible that both the woman and myself might have had some choice in the matter had we been consulted. The Sister seated the stranger next to me, saying that she would explain later. But I wish to remark to you, my friend, that I have never been harmed by my contact with that 'San Francisco woman,' as you call her. She has taught me some valuable lessons, as have some others that I could mention." Here I looked at her sharply.

"Now don't be angry with me," she said, snuggling up to me and hanging on to me with both hands. "You know, dear," she said, looking up into my face with a childlike smile most exasperating, "that we cannot be angry up here on account of our Spirits; you must remember what Father Hyacinth said about angry passions."

"True! true! But did he say something about disgust?" I replied. "I am simply disgusted with your style. You see, Annie," I continued, "since that morning that Sister Alicia seated that woman near me, taking her away from your side, I have studied her very closely to see if I could find out why the change was made. I have discovered that she is very finely educated, and unusually considerate of the rights and feelings of others. I have never seen her do a selfish act. I have grown to esteem her highly; and John says that she is an 'Advanced Thinker.' I do not know exactly what he means by that, but something good, I know. And, my dear, I think that she can instruct us both in many things good for us to know, even if she does wear ugly dresses."

Annie was silent for some moments, not looking up, but digging up the soil with the toe of her boot.

At length she said, "But don't you believe that certain individuals exhale a poisonous atmosphere, and that some are actually surrounded by evil spirits? You remember in the lesson last evening, concerning Mary Magdalene, it appears that she kept seven devils on hand all the time, at one period of her experience. I believe every word that Father Hyacinth said this morning," turning and looking me full in the face. "I should think you would understand the thing by this time."

"I do," I replied, "believe every word of it. I feel sure that there are devils hanging about people, as in the days of Mary Magdalene, and that some must have unholy and unclean atmospheres. But there it is again; Brother Paul told me this morning that we couldn't safely judge another without convicting ourselves, that we can never see in another what we have not experienced ourselves; in fact, we could not see a devil in another without having known how it was ourselves."

We walked on in silence for some minutes, I asking my soul how much of the law of Love I had exemplified in my morning's work, and I thought,

"Lord God of Hosts, be with us yet,
    Lest we forget—
    Lest we forget!"

Here Annie squared herself around, and taking my face between her two hands, looked me straight in the eyes for a minute, at last she said, "Elizabeth, you are correct; I have the devil in me sometimes I know, but I don't want to be bad. I am going to ask Father Hyacinth to try and regenerate me. He says it can be done if I will only give myself up to the Spirit. Now what does he mean? You think I have too many Spirits already, don't you?"

"It all depends upon what sort you give yourself up to," I answered, as we entered the spacious dining room, and took in, not only the delicious fragrance of the fruit and flowers, but the mental and spiritual aura of the noble souls there assembled.

Annie pressed close to me and whispered, "I never felt it before!"

CHAPTER V.

Benares, California, May 18th.

As I carefully note the perfect system governing this colony, the great amount of labor accomplished, and the ease and perfection with which it is done; the unfailing consideration, love and devotion manifested among the members; the absolute liberty granted to all, I am led to the conclusion that this is a practical demonstration of an ideal brotherhood.

At first the teachings of Father Hyacinth did not appeal to me; they were so new, and so unlike anything that I had ever heard or read of, but gradually they began to assume some form and proportion, until now it seems to me that I have known all of these things somewhere before. Where previously I had been an incessant talker all my life, I have now grown more reserved, silent and eager to hear and observe. As I take a retrospect of my past life it all appears so utterly empty and foolish that I am led to wonder how John could ever have been so patient and gentle with me.

This is such a beautiful world up here. The grand mountain scenery, the highly cultivated valley, the symmetrical and artistic buildings, the color and harmony, all go to delight the lover of the beautiful. Everything is done with an eye to beauty as well as utility.

Annie and I have asked the privilege of occasionally accompanying the Brothers and Sisters in their rounds of duty; in the orchards with the fruit pickers, in the store rooms where the delicious and perfect fruit is assorted and crated and made ready for shipping. Annie declares that she knows the fruit up in that old garden, which Eve made such a blunder over, wasn't any nicer than the car loads that are daily shipped from this plantation.

Brother Paul has a way of looking at the girl when she gets on her talking moods that tones her down, especially when he asks her, in his slow way, if she isn't afraid that she is talking too much. She never knows how to talk back to him. Nearly everyone else gets a touch of her wit or sarcasm, but just one glance from that man is enough to, at least, change the nature of her talk; yet his marvelous eyes cheer, comfort and strengthen whenever occasion calls. Brother Paul is a study. He is altogether lovely—if one can safely say that of a masculine member of the human family.

But then the entire association manifests that same peculiarity; a species of reserve power that is felt at once upon entering the presence of any members of the family. There is something so sweet and attractive about them that you instinctively want to turn and follow them as they are passing you in their round of duty. This peculiar attractiveness is universal with all; it is something that I have never sensed in any other body of people I ever came in contact with. I have on rare occasions met an individual possessing such power, but not perhaps more than one out of a thousand.

I mentioned this singular fact to Brother Frederick, and after studying me intently for a time, he said that I would understand the secret of all this later on, but that one cause of the serenity and cheerfulness characterizing the whole colony was because they were non-flesh-eating.

"We consider," he continued, "that the consumption of large quantities of oft times diseased flesh must cause, to some degree, a putrescent state of the blood in the human being, giving rise to that offensive odor which is constantly being exhaled from the body, also causing that irritability and violence of temper so common in the world."

Here Annie nudged me, and whispered, "Now I understand why I am becoming such an angel; it is because I don't eat meat."

This morning while out walking we stopped and watched the Brothers as they were turning on the water to irrigate the valley. I asked one of them, who was standing near me, if they ever had any kind of sickness in the colony.

"No; why should we?" he answered.

"Don't all people get sick sometimes?" I asked.

"Well, we do not believe in it; we never speak the word. We deny that there is such a thing in reality. We never think of such things; never talk about them. There is so much that is good and lovely crowded in upon us, that we have no time to think of anything that is not Good. We constantly deny all that you name Evil; and what we do not desire we simply decline."

Here Annie, who was standing with open eyes and mouth, asked, "Why! do you never expect to get sick up here? and never expect to die?"

"We all expect to pass through that change which you people talk of so much and call death," answered the Brother gently, "but we do not expect sickness, neither will we have it."

"Now that reminds me of something," cried Annie; "I have not seen anything like a burial ground or vault. What do you do with your people when they 'pass out,' as you call it?"

"Cremation is our method of disposing of the remains of both the human and the animal," the Brother replied.

"Worse and worse!" exclaimed Annie, turning abruptly and walking away hurriedly.

"Do you know," she said, as I joined her a few moments later, "that these people are regular heathens!"

"I wish there were more like them; the world would be the better, I am sure," I replied.

We walked along in silence for some moments until we came to the entrance of their immense apiary, which was under the care of six of the Sisters. Sister Alicia was about to enter, so she invited us to go in with her.

This branch of their industry is intensely interesting. The study of bee life and intelligence possesses a greater fascination to me than any other department in this colossal enterprise. I need not enlarge upon the beauty and excellence of their product, as everyone is familiar with the fame of California honey.

In my eagerness to study the working of the colonies of bees about to swarm, I had forgotten all about Annie. When I began to look about for her, one of the Sisters said laughingly, "Oh! she made her escape long ago. Strangers rarely dare to come in among the hives, especially during their swarming season. Bees are very sensitive to odors and auras. They don't appear to mind you however."

When I reached the Home I found Annie, with a flushed face, laying down the law to one of the Brothers who was cleaning the porches. As I came up she turned, blazing with anger, and shaking her small fist at me, cried out, "You must have been in a bad way for entertainment to go in among those little wretches. Just look at my hand! I'll never touch another drop of honey as long as I live. I'll kill every bee that I can get at; the horrid things!"

"I am sorry for that, for really honey is a large part of our living," said a low voice near by.

We turned and there stood Brother Paul and John. I did not look in the face of either of the men, for I was just ready to cry myself for having taken the child into danger; but Annie walked straight up to John and laid her wounded hand into his great strong one.

He did not say anything for some moments, but just passed his soft magnetic fingers over the swollen parts. At last he said, "Don't you see, dear, that it is nothing to lose one's temper over? don't you see that the whole thing is gone?" Sure enough, the swelling had nearly disappeared.

I now looked up at Brother Paul. He was simply looking at the girl, and she had quieted down and was smiling, quite her old self again.

As I looked at the group standing silent and motionless, I recalled to mind many things I had seen John do at home, and had considered it all nonsense; now I could not deny the fact that a great change had come over Annie, and that her hand appeared to be all right, as far as I could see. At all events, from a state of uncontrollable anger, she had passed into one of peace and serenity, all in the space of a few moments; an unusual thing for her. Generally in her fits she kicked and floundered around for an hour or two, until I could in some way pacify her; after which she would be so sweet and charming and altogether lovely that one would forget how confoundedly disagreeable she had been.

I slyly stole away out of sight, for I felt that it was a scene too sacred for an outsider to intrude upon. Then, too, I considered myself in fault somehow for the unpleasant affair, and now, as I wandered off under the shadow of the great trees I kept asking myself, "How is it done? Do they do it, or is it because she behaves herself?" Then I recalled how Christ stilled the tempest, cast out devils, healed the sick, gave sight to the blind, etc. "Yes," I thought, "but He was Christ. Can those things be done in these days by human beings?"

I took my pocket Testament out and opened it; and the first thing I found rather startled me, it was this: "These twelve Jesus sent forth, and commanded them, saying, Go, heal the sick, cleanse the lepers, raise the dead, cast out devils." These men were as common and earthly as any we have in these days, it seems to me. I thought of John, and Brother Paul, and, goodness! there is Father Hyacinth; to say nothing of the rest of these honest, earnest men and women who are trying so hard to follow Christ's law.

I pondered over this matter long and earnestly, hidden away as I was out of sight of humanity. It was hard to accept the idea that those two men possessed some power for good over that wayward girl that I did not. "If they can do it, I don't see why I can't," I muttered to myself.

Then I opened my Testament again, and presently I came on this passage: "Indeed, I assure you, he believing on me, the works which I do, shall he do also; and greater than these shall he do. And whatever you may ask in my name, that will I do."

"I think I understand how the thing is done," I said aloud, as I rose and started homeward, reaching the Home just as the family was being seated at the dinner table.

Annie looked supremely happy, seated next to John, presenting no vestage of the mental cyclone that had so lately wrenched and distorted her.

Brother Rameses, seeing that I was alone, beckoned me to a seat next to him, which I gladly accepted, feeling at once rested and comforted. This man is no talker, unless he has something to say, but he can quote poetry day in and day out. I cannot say that I care for poetry as a general thing. As I, from time to time, looked up to the grave face, with its clean shaven, square cut chin, clear, honest blue eyes, and massive brows shaded by a wealth of yellow hair, a kind of an awe crept over me; I almost wished he wasn't so solid, wasn't so awfully good.

Presently he turned and looked down at me, saying, "Had rather an interesting episode this morning, eh?"

I knew he had reference to the bee tragedy, so I never answered.

Then he let out on his poetry.

"A fool there was, and he made his prayer
(Even as you and I!)
To a rag and a bone and a hank of hair,
We called her the woman, who did not care
But the fool, he called her his lady fair
(Even as you and I)" *

"Oh, the years we waste and the tears we waste,
And the work of our head and hand
Belong to the woman who did not know
And now we know, that she never could know
And did not understand." *

We sat long in silence, until I began to boil inwardly. "Well, that is not very interesting— not much poetry in that," I blurted out. It always made me savage to hear a man say anything in a slighting way concerning a woman, no matter what I might think or know.

"Why! that is an effusion of the prospective poet-laureate of England," said Rameses, after a silence, as he peeled and quartered a luscious orange and laid it on my plate.

* Kipling.

I was silent during the remainder of the meal, but I could see that the man was studying me, and could feel a thrill go all over me—a new sensation to me, and one that I did not understand.

As we arose from the table Father Hyacinth came forward to where we were, and said to Rameses, "I would like to speak with you for a few moments if you are at liberty."

My companion excused himself, and bowing to me with a stately dignity passed on out of sight.

I walked out on the lawn in a brown study. I was really a little anxious concerning my sentiments regarding that yellow-haired Austrian. There are some things about these men up here that one likes awfully well; and some things that you don't like at all. I must talk with John about it.

"This visible universe is composed of invisible non-contiguous atoms; it rests on space, but the ruling forces themselves are immaterial and invisible. Seek matter and you will not find it; it is mirage that recedes as you advance; it is a shadow that vanishes each time you think to seize it."

—Camille Flammarion.

FIFTH LESSON.

COSMIC LIFE.

The object of urging this ponderous subject upon the attention of this class is not merely for the pleasure which the knowledge brings for the time, but for the important influence which an understanding of and an obedience to the divine law must exert upon the life and character of the individual; and really not alone upon the individual man, but upon all manifested life. Inasmuch as man, through his transgression, caused all the disasters that now curse the race and the planet, it devolves upon him to adjust those disjointed conditions in the lower kingdoms; as the healing of the low fierce brute life, and the diseased vegetable world, can come only through redeemed humanity.

Paul appears to have had a perfect understanding of this great truth. He says:

"Indeed the earnest expectation of creation longs for the revelation of the 'Sons of God.' For the creation was made subject to frailty.

* * * in the hope that even the creation itself will become emancipated from the slavery of corruption into the freedom of the glory of the children of God.

"For we know that the whole creation groaneth and travaileth in pain together till the present time.

"For the creation was made subject to frailty."

This idea will not appear so strange and unreasonable when we understand the nature of the Life principle of the universe, which is not a structureless substance, an invisible nothing, but a vast ocean of infinitesimal atoms, each possessing in itself a power of expansion too mighty for the human mind to comprehend.

In the original and perfect state, this cosmic Substance surrounding our planet was composed, as we have seen, of atoms, each of which was double, possessing two distinct lives, male and female, in one atom,—the divine marriage. So that everything created of, or growing out of, this great body of Life was dual, until the sex sin came.

Those tiny bodies compose that shoreless sea of Substance—for it is substance—from which is evolved all objective life; and into that great reservoir of exhaustless Substance these atoms return, to be again and again called out to form new and more beautiful objects.

There is but one Substance, from which is created all of the changing forms which men have named Matter.

"Because everything exists from the beginning in God, into whose unmanifested state all things will return. * *
* * There is no death in nature, and the dying of the beings consists in their return to the body of their Mother. That is to say, in an extinction and suppression of one form of existence and activity, in a re-birth of the same thing * * * in a new form, possessed of new faculties that are adapted to its new surroundings."

—Paracelsus.

This Substance, like its Infinite Source, is deathless. Those appearances which men have named Death and Decay are not in the Substance itself, but are merely dissolving views of the forms and shapes fashioned from it.

Its fixed character for the time has been changed, so that there exists in all visible things a restlessness, a constant impulse toward change. The atoms still feel the stress of the divine law of duality that once ruled them, and are therefore moving hither and thither seeking and desiring the divine union again. This condition causes that nameless longing and constant desire for change that marks the character of the race today, and which might be classed as a species of insanity.

Prof. F. R. Japp, one of the foremost scientists of the world, in his address before the chemical section of the British Association, his subject being, "The Life resident in the Atomic Substance; the Ceaseless Activity of the Atoms; their Attraction and Repulsion," said, "The absolute origin of the compounds of one-sided asymmetry to be found in the living world is a mystery as profound as the absolute origin of life itself."

"An asymmetric compound is one which is not complete and evenly balanced, and which, because of its incompleteness, seeks to ally itself with its chemical affinity and therefore continues in a condition of restless activity."*

Through the infusion of the virus of the animal sex-life into the atomic Substance there came a violent shock, the wrenching asunder of

* The Pantheism of Modern Science.

that holy union in the atoms; so that instead of there being in one atom two nucleoli or germs, there is now but a single germ in each, a male or female, as the case may be; a negative or positive, as the scientist terms them. There is now a constant warfare in that portion of the substance that goes to make up man and his planet; his Substance of Life has lost its steadfastness, has come under the law of limitation— a man-made law.

Although this Substance received a shock that has changed its action, it is still indestructible and redeemable.

The violation of the spiritual law of reproduction of the human family, and the externalization of the sex-life on the animal plane, produced a marked change in all of the kingdoms of the earth, and upon the body of the planet itself. "The earth is also defiled under the inhabitants thereof; because they have transgressed the law, broken the everlasting covenant."

Before man broke that law, the vegetable world was without disease or blight. Those animals that are now so destructive to all forms of life were then unknown; there was nothing to hurt or make afraid. But when he disobeyed and "ate of that tree of the knowledge of good and evil," then began his degeneracy and the infusing of that lust-poison into the Life Substance enveloping our planet.

"Cursed is the ground for thy sake; * * * thorns also and thistles shall it bring forth to thee." This was not a curse, for divine love cannot curse. It was a prophecy. A divine law had been broken and there is no forgiveness of sin.

"Thou shalt not eat of it; for in the day that thou eatest thereof thou shalt surely die." Not to die, as we know death, but the sowing of the seed of decay, dissolution and discord. The larger portion of the earth's surface is at this time a barren waste; nay, worse than that! it is in a condition that breeds suffering and death to the thousands who are forced to inhabit it. "Cursed is the ground for thy sake, in sorrow shalt thou eat of it."

Every atom composing the vast sea of Life is sentient. Each recognizes and responds to each. Man is an aggregation of these atoms; he vitally influences the whole mass surrounding him; his thoughts act upon this sea of Life as a solid and foreign substance would upon a body of water. If a pebble be thrown into a placid lake it will agitate the entire body to its extreme limit, every molecule feeling the vibration. The more powerful the disturbing influence, the greater the agitation.

The great atomic sea of Life is One, and the thoughts of intelligent beings strongly influences the responsive medium for good or evil. All beligerent thoughts, evil and brutal passions, disturb that spiritual atmosphere so that equilibrium is lost, the vibrations become irregular and at times violent.

It appears evident enough from the study of all ancient religious history, to say nothing of proofs of geology, that our planet has, at one time, received a terrible shock, and that the orbit of the earth has been changed from interstellar space to its present position. We need only to bear in mind that worlds are not stationary, but float upon an elastic sea, whose Substance responds to the thoughts of God-created beings. There can be no question but that our planet, from its weight of crime, bloodshed and wrong, has sunk in space, as a stone would sink in water; and through the united weight of the rebellious mind of the race swung gradually out of its original orbit, and away from the great Central Sun of the universe.

Those terrific mental cyclones that have swept

the face of the globe from age to age certainly must have influenced adversely its position and motion on that shoreless and responsive ocean.

Attraction and repulsion are the two great motive powers of the universe.

We will not forget that Mind is the creative power. Certain states of mind are repellent and destructive. Denial of God and the Good is a form of blasphemy. At all times, the spirit of hatred expressed, it matters not toward whom, has the power to repel, to drive from the Good. All selfishness, denial of the Christ, hatred of our kind, anger and jealousy, has a tendency to drive us still further from that Central Life—our source. Denial is death—repulsion. While on the other hand all affirmations for the Good; love for man, and all that lives; adoration for the divine Source of Life; obedience to the Christ, to love as He loved, is the positive magnet that will attract all toward the light.

When we take into consideration the fact that at one period of the world's history evil reigned supreme, the whole race being in darkness, it will not appear so unreasonable or strange that the united sins of blasphemous people could cause our world to fall from its high estate.

From time immemorial, men have preached about the "fall of man," but have never said anything about the "fallen world;" yet the world received its due share of the curse.

"God saw everything that He had made, and behold it was very good." We have perfect faith that God never made a mistake; never made a botch. It is not consistent with divine wisdom, harmony, justice, or love, that He should have created so imperfect a piece of work as our planet and its inhabitants. That He should have thrown us off in this isolated corner of the universe with no near companions, save a dead moon and a rapidly consuming sun; when there appears to be a region of space filled with myriads of glowing suns, a great pathway of eternal day, where there must be light and warmth and consequent happiness. Darkness and cold is where God is not, and brings to man his greatest suffering.

Neither can I believe that the divine Architect ever left our globe so tipped upon its axis that so large a portion of its habitable surface is beyond the reach of warmth, light and comfort. While we—in this so-called garden of the world—are in darkness half of the twenty-four hours which constitutes our day; a period during which are perpetrated the vilest and most diabolical of crimes, that daily shock the reading public.

And God said, "Let there be light." God the infinite Lover, the infinite Good, never created anything adverse to Himself. He is love, light, fire and eternal life. Cold and darkness come from man's denial of God, and resistance of the Good.

Our planet in its first estate, doubtless, was one of that mighty procession of suns in what we call the Milky Way, up toward which we gaze night after night with deep reverence and much questioning.

But we are told that there was war in heaven. "How art thou fallen from heaven, O Lucifer, son of the morning!" The disobedience, crime, cruelty and bloodshed of mankind acted as a repelling force, causing our planet to sink from that belt of light, heat and love, down to its present level.

It all came through the law of repulsion. Good does not love Evil, and Evil hates Good. There was, therefore, a mutual repulsion. Nothing has occurred outside of a fixed and unyielding law, and wholly in harmony with divine dynamics.

From our sacred history we glean the following, all going to substantiate our claim.

"For behold, the Lord cometh out of his place to punish the inhabitants of the earth for their iniquity. The earth also shall disclose her blood, and shall no more cover her slain.

"I will punish the world for their evil. * * * Therefore I will shake the heavens, and the earth shall remove out of her place.

"Behold the Lord maketh the earth empty and maketh it waste, and turneth it upside down.

"The earth shall reel to and fro like a drunkard.

"The earth is utterly broken down. * * * The earth is moved exceedingly. * * * * And shall be removed like a cottage; and the transgression thereof shall be heavy upon it; and it shall fall.

"The land shall be utterly emptied, and utterly spoiled, for the Lord hath spoken this word. * * * * Upon the land of my people shall come up thorns and briers."

Life would be utterly bereft of its incentive were we not assured that the Good is an eternal principle, and Evil but a passing dream, a nightmare, a mirage.

We are promised a divine panacea for the

transient malady now torturing the soul Substance of things. "And the inhabitants shall not say, I am sick, * * * for the Lord is our judge, the Lord is our law-giver, the Lord is our King; He will save us."

Our Lord came not alone to heal the sick soul of things; but to establish an electric chain between our planet and the Central Sun of our system, to assist in attracting the globe into its original position and place in that "Home of the many Mansions" in that pathway of light.

We with our darkened vision cannot see that wondrous chain of light over which, passing and re-passing, are hosts of angelic beings, who, with Christ's love in their souls, are aiding in the work of redeeming man and his disjointed world. Ages ago, Jacob, on his pillow of stone, saw in a vision that ladder of light let down amid the blackness.

Christ said, "I say unto you, that hereafter you shall see the heavens open, and the angels of God ascending and descending to the Son of man."

There are now a few advanced minds investigating this science, and who understand the almighty force resident in atomic Life. This force —or power—under the control of the divine

Mind in man, supported by the will, could sway a planet in its course, as wind can a thistledown.

I have perfect confidence in the lessons of my Master and Teacher. He said, "He that believeth on Me, the works that I do shall he do also; and greater works than these shall he do. * * * If you should say to this mountain, Be thou lifted up and thrown into the sea; it will be done. And whatever you shall ask in prayer, believing, you will receive."

Prayer, we understand, is nothing but an earnest desire. The time is not distant when men and women, wise, just and Godly, mighty in thought and will, having a practical knowledge of this unseen power, can employ it for the reinstatement of human affairs in our world; just as readily as men, who have come into an understanding of electricity can utilize that subtle power for the benefit of mankind.

"You shall know the truth, and the truth shall make you free."

What is this truth? Is it not the secret of this Life Substance of which we have been speaking, and our intimate relation to it? All Life is One, and we have each done our share in the degradation of the whole. We are therefore called upon individually to assist in this wonderful work of restoration.

What are we to do in a work so mighty, and we so weak?

Are we weak? We have for our central force the Christ-Mind, the God within us. From that source our thoughts are deathless, and we impress for Good the ocean of ether in which we exist. He who thinks a loving thought has lightened the burden of the world.

Divine Love, like divine Life, is a Substance; it enters into the ocean of life and heals the wound of sins; it unites the severed lives in the atoms.

Christ was the Substance of Love itself. We are His children; His helpers. We are to establish on earth that "kingdom of Good,"—the kingdom of divine Love. Our thoughts must be as grappling irons thrown out to anchor and steady our world in her erratic and troubled homeward journey.

The millennial dawn may not be as distant as we are disposed to think, when we take into consideration the marvelous speed in the movement of our entire planetary system; and understand that all of the starry hosts are being whirled through space toward some great center at a speed incomprehensible to the human mind.

During the past century, yes, during the last decade, man has demonstrated fully his power for good over the earth's surface; making the "waste places blossom like the rose." The earth materializes the thoughts of mankind, be they what they may.

Not only is man subduing the surface of the globe, but he is learning to master the secret forces as well. These demonstrations are all in their infancy; yet they substantiate our apparently extravagant claims for the race.

We can now dimly comprehend the meaning of that promise:

"They shall not hurt, nor destroy, in all my holy mountains; for the earth shall be full of the knowledge of the Lord, as water covereth the deep."

"All things that my Father hath are mine, nothing shall wrest them from Me." "I am the light of the world." "These things I command you; that you love one another."

And this divine Lover of Souls has instructed me that I am my brother's keeper, and that my brother is to be as dear to me as myself; in fact, that I must give myself for his good if required;

and that all men of whatever grade, color, condition or clime are my brethren.

He has also in His tender love told me that I must keep watch for the returning prodigal, and that when I see him afar off, that I must hasten to meet him, lest he think himself unwelcome and turn back.

"And I saw a new heaven and a new earth; for the first heaven and the first earth were passed away; and there was no more sea.

"And I, John, saw the holy city, new Jerusalem, coming down from God out of heaven, prepared as a bride adorned for her husband. And I heard a great voice out of heaven saying, "Behold, the tabernacle of God is with men, and He will dwell with them, and they shall be His people, and God himself shall be with them, and be their God. And God shall wipe away all tears from their eyes; and there shall be no more death, neither sorrow nor crying, neither shall there be any more pain, for the former things are passed away.

"And He that sat upon the throne said, Behold, I make all things new. And He said unto me, Write, for these words are true and faithful.

"And He said unto me, It is done. I am Alpha

and Omega, the beginning and the end. I will give unto him that is athirst of the fountain of the water of life freely. He that overcometh, shall inherit all things; and I will be his God, and he shall be my son."

CHAPTER VI.

· Benares, California, June 2d.

Today, thirteen persons, old and young, male and female, came to the Home on the eleven o'clock train. So quietly is everything conducted in this institution that no one outside of the regular family knew anything of the matter; so that we visitors were quite excited over the arrivals.

As Angela and I were watching the new comers file up the steps and enter the hall, we hailed Sister Alicia, who was passing near where we were seated, and asked her what she was going to do with her new recruits.

"Come with me, and see for yourselves," she answered, looking back over her shoulder smiling and showing her white teeth and dimples.

We followed her upstairs and through a set of hallways entirely new to us, as we had never investigated that wing of the Home building.

"We have four hundred available sleeping

rooms in this city," she said, with an air of satisfaction; "and every one of them comfortably if not handsomely furnished; quite as much so as these," opening a door into a suite of large, airy rooms, all tastefully and artistically furnished, and immaculately clean. "We are never taken by surprise up here; we keep 'open house' at all times, and many of those who have been called 'tramps' find their way to us. I may say all of whom stay with us permanently, trusted and beloved. We have in our brotherhood members from almost every civilized nation on the globe."

"I suppose you must have suitable rooms for your working people and tramps," I suggested, as we inspected suites of really handsome rooms with their polished floors and large windows.

The Sister was silent for a moment, then in her quiet impressive way said, "We make no distinction here; our 'working people,' as you call them, are all equal, we have no grades; if we ever show any preference it is toward those who have been unfortunate in some way. As for our 'tramps,' we should not do better by royalty. We desire to make them forget all past grades and misfortunes; and we succeed usually."

There was something in her quiet tone and manner that humbled me, and started me on a train of thought not altogether flattering to my self-love. And as she and Angela walked on in advance of me, talking over the arrangement of the buildings, I followed slowly, thinking of tramp life, and not feeling quite comfortable, not knowing in fact who my near neighbors might be.

Then I recalled the history and nature of that tramp which the dear old bishop put into the spare bed room; and I remembered the silver candle-sticks, and all that grew out of the bishop's kindness, confidence and patience toward that despised and hunted convict; the influence for good on all the after life of that brutal tramp. And as I thought of Him who ate with publicans and sinners and was not harmed; who labored among the down-trodden and sinful in order to elevate and save; there came to me a dim consciousness of the oneness of humanity. I recalled all of John's schemes and exploits with tramps, depraved and outcasts of all creation. I remembered how I had ridiculed and abused him for his patience and confidence toward what I had considered and termed the "rough scuffs" of all creation. Now there was unrolled before me a picture of the vast multitudes of the friendless, homeless and outcast of the human family, and I saw walking in advance of that multitude that One, who said, "Inasmuch as you do it unto the least of these, you have done it unto me." Then came over me such a wave of compassion that for a moment I was stunned; I had never realized before that so large a majority of the race were among those "little ones."

This new question must have impressed itself in a degree upon my face, for when I came up to where Sister Alicia and Angela were awaiting me they both looked at me sharply, and Angela passing her arm about me smilingly said, "Of one blood made He all, my dear."

We now entered a suite of rooms which Sister Alicia had selected for a party. She informed us that four out of the party of thirteen—two gentlemen and two ladies—were from England, and were of English aristocracy: Sir Anthony Westlake, his wife and daughter, and Sir Charles Westlake, Sir Anthony's brother. The remaining party were from San Francisco, and were friends of the "San Francisco woman," as Annie called her. They consisted of two gentlemen and their wives, and five single ladies.

"These people who come in on trial, do the husbands and wives live in the old relations," asked Angela.

"No," Sister Alicia answered; "they conform to our rules in regard to those relations, and if at the close of their season of trial they should not consider themselves ready to adopt the permanent life of celibacy, they return to their homes, none the worse for their sojourn with us. But in the experience of half a century there have been but two cases where the parties have deemed it best to renew their old relations."

At dinner the English party was seated at our table, and next to Angela. It appears they had been many years in India, in the same section where Angela spent so much time. They were familiar with all the occult philosophies, and had made a thorough study of Theosophy. This fact at once made a tie between the party and Angela. The young baronet and John fairly tumbled into each other's affections. We were all refreshed by the new element coming in.

Annie whispered to me, as we were leaving the dining room, "I am going to set my cap for that young lord. He is a 'catch,' and I am amazingly fond of lords."

"I trust that you will behave with becoming dignity," I said, looking at her soberly.

"I could not do otherwise, with you as my example," she replied meekly.

The most delightful occasion of the day is the reunion on the lawn after the evening meal; the entire family gathers, forming an altogether unique group, charming beyond anything that could be imagined.

Supper is served promptly at five o'clock; then while the Sisters are arranging domestic matters in the house, the Brothers are milking, straining the milk, putting it in the coolers, and taking care of the stock; and by half past six the whole family, including the guests, are ready for the evening pastime, which consists of music, reading or speaking. As a rule, this gathering takes place on the lawn, as we never have rain here, and the air is so delightful.

From six until seven o'clock we are to have music this evening, furnished by Brother Rameses with his violin, and the Sisters with their stringed instruments.

I find it impossible to describe the quality or the effect of the music in this strange out-of-the-way place, under those old red-wood trees, with the grand mountain scenery rising up beyond the reach of human vision as a back ground; then in front, stretching away as far as the eye can reach, the fertile valley, smooth and regular, with its various shades and colors, forming an extended picture of rich fruitage, and all about the signs of high civilization without the slash and clang that accompanies it. As I sat entranced by the music and the scenery I questioned in my mind if they really had anything better on the planet Mars.

In looking over the grounds while the people were seating themselves, I could not help noting the general air of cheerfulness and good humor pervading the whole assembly. I could not define the difference between that gathering and hundreds of others that I had been in. There were over three hundred persons on the lawn, yet there was no noise or confusion; but instead a kind of subdued gayety, quite new to me; all of the faces shone with a species of good humor and good will toward each other. I had always been of the rollicking sort, and Annie even more so, when in her best moods.

As I looked over the company, I espied Annie seated beside Sir Charles, deeply engaged in highly animated conversation.

My attention was now drawn toward the stage by the arrival of Rameses and his troupe.

As I sat, entranced by the music, in that most charming and secluded spot, having for my companions so many choice spirits, I in my own enthusiastic way sent up a kind of petition that this curious people with their strange doctrines and wholesome and righteous living might become known and emulated by the world at large.

It appears that Sir Anthony Westlake had casually remarked to Brother Frederick that doubtless this fraternity would, in time, go the way of all similar institutions; so it had been considered wise that some one should explain briefly wherein this colony differed from all others that have risen and declined from time to time. Brother Rameses was chosen to make this explanation at the close of the concert. I was astonished beyond measure, as I had never heard that gigantic Australian utter a dozen words, except to recite poetry, at which he was an adept.

I looked enquiringly at John, who nodded toward the man, as much as to say that he was all right.

Rameses arose with a dignity and ease of manner rarely displayed by an occasional speaker, and in a quiet deliberate way—in much the same manner as he draws his bow across his violin when he brings out such heavenly music —he spoke as follows:

"I have been asked to explain in few words the

foundation principles of our fraternity. I have had a somewhat intimate acquaintance with many of the schools and fraternities that have sprung up at different times in different countries. From my early boyhood I had conceived of an ideal brotherhood, composed of both men and women on an equal footing; an institution that should be a school possessing all the facilities for a first class education, where those who had been neglected in their childhood could receive a mental and physical training that would develop the best that was in them, regardless of sex, age, nationality or color.

"I have entered many different fraternities, and after studying carefully their foundation tenets, have retired from them, having failed to find what I deemed to be the true foundation for a lasting corporation, that is self-governing and altruistic. All fraternities that I have come in contact with have been under the dominance of some strong leading spirit, who possessed both a mind and will of the strongest order, and who in many cases exerted a hypnotic influence over all that it came in contact with. All bodies thus governed endure but a brief season after the leading mind has been withdrawn.

"This brotherhood has no leader. Never has

had one; at least, not in the form of man. We all remember that He whom we accept as our Leader and Counsellor, said, 'He that would be first among you, let him be last.' There is not one in this brotherhood that is esteemed above another. Every important move to be made is submitted to the whole body, male and female alike. There are those in the fraternity whose judgment we prize, and whose wisdom we revere, but such never attempt to lead.

"When you take into consideration the fact that this city up here on the mountain side, with all of its grand and massive buildings so exquisitely finished, is entirely the work of the members of this brotherhood, you will be compelled to acknowledge that we have talent of a superior order among our members, much of which has been developed wholly in our schools.

"Those members who have been deprived of opportunity for education in youth enter our schools as children, and are carefully taught and developed, so that there are none more highly favored than others. We have several hundred members in our colony, but there is not one who does not know every screw in this vast machinery, and who would not be capable of coming to the front if need be.

"Men and women to enter this colony must become capable. It is an educational institution; a great body of men and women who live up to wise and just principles; therefore it must continue, altruism being the foundation of the whole fabric.

"But the most potent reason for the lasting nature of this brotherhood is the position we give our women. We have equal suffrage here. We know that women are going to lead in all works of reform. Woman has never lost her stamp of the Divine, therefore we place her foremost in the ranks of honor. We venerate, and try to emulate her. We remember that she was the last to leave our Lord at His crucifixion, and the first to meet Him at His resurrection. We consider her the advance guard of the race, and if you watch carefully you will see that this is not all talk with us. We believe with our Mahatma, 'The word which shall come to save the world shall be uttered by a woman.''

"But we speak the wisdom of God, which was hidden in a mystery, and which God previously designed, before the ages, for our glory. But wisdom, not of this age nor of those rulers of this age, who are coming to an end."

"Now we have received, not the spirit of the world, but that Spirit which is from God, that we may know the things graciously given to us by God; and which things we speak, not in words taught by human wisdom, but the teachings of the Spirit; unfolding spiritual things."

"Now the animal man does not receive the things of the Spirit of God, for they are foolishness to him; and he is not able to understand. because they are spiritually examined."

"But we possess the Mind of Christ."

—I. Corinthians ii.

"The Spirit of the Lord is upon me, because He hath anointed me to proclaim glad tidings to the poor, He hath sent me to publish release to the captive and recovery of sight to the blind; to dispense freedom to the oppressed, and proclaim an era of acceptance with the Lord."

—Gospel of our Lord.

"The people that walked in darkness have seen a great light; they that dwelt in the land of the shadow of death, upon them hath the light shined."

—Isaiah.

SIXTH LESSON.

CHRIST'S MISSION.

Christ did not come into the world simply as a teacher to mankind, or as a demonstration of the redeemed Man, of which He was so perfect a type; but as the great Healer, not alone of man and the planet, but of that sea of cosmic Substance from which objective life is formed.

The redeeming quality of Christ's blood and body has always been the chief corner-stone in the Christian religion. However the various sects may differ on other points, they steadfastly adhere to the one crowning glory, the redeeming power of Christ's body and blood.

Through what channels and by what means that healing and redeeming process was accomplished has never been satisfactorily explained; at least not in these later days. That old story that Christ was sacrificed to appease the wrath of an angry God, in order that a comparatively few out of the great hosts of human beings might see salvation from endless punishment, is as a body of religious teachings most repulsive to the humane and thoughtful seeker after truth. To such this teaching has for a foundation neither reason nor justice.

There is abroad at this time a strong spirit of inquiry, a desire to ferret out hidden things, which, if they be based upon science or reason, can be readily comprehended by the reasoning and thinking individual.

Gods works through laws and by orderly methods, and not through miracles or especial providences. The whole tenor of the life of Christ ran to a purpose. All things were ordered to be just as they were; but not for signs or symbols, any more than the general preparation for the laying of the Atlantic cable, or the stretching of our telegraph wires, were intended as symbols of the completed works. Christ's birth was no miracle. His life and His death were controlled by laws; the whole process was scientific and methodical. He came to perform an important work, and He did it according to fixed laws.

Mankind, through sin, corruption and selfishness, had sunk so low in the scale of being as to be in danger of annihilation; not only was man himself in jeopardy, but the planet was in a state of collapse from its weight of crime.

Christ having called man and the planet into objective existence, it devolved upon Him to watch over and protect His work, which was only in accordance with divine justice. God's pity and love saw a way through which the race and planet could be redeemed and restored to their primitive purity and perfection. And because of His intimate relations with mankind, Christ was chosen to take upon Himself the healing and restoring of the world.

This could only be accomplished through His coming to our planet, associating Himself with its interests; and assuming the human form, thereby connecting Himself with the race and establishing an electric union between our sorrowful world and that belt of light toward which we gaze and for which we yearn.

Christ being of immaculate birth, His body and blood was composed, as we have seen, of the imperishable Substance. The dual atoms composing it possessed within themselves an incalculable capacity for expansion, increase and healing. There was but one avenue through which this healing life could be brought into immediate contact with the life of the earth and the human family.

It is an established fact in history that crucifixion was the general mode of executing malefactors in the time of Christ; it is also known that it was a bloodless method of taking life, Christ being an exception; He was lacerated and torn; He was "Christ of the seven wounds." He literally shed His blood, all of which was according to a plan. Every drop of that immaculate blood, by a process incomprehensible to us, was absorbed into the sick and tortured soul of the planet, where it has through all of these centuries been healing the sting of sin.

This theory will not appear strange or unreasonable when we take into consideration the fact that there is no such thing as Matter, as generally understood, but that Spirit is the only Substance in the universe, and that Christ's body and blood was of this Substance in its unpolluted state.

He, while on earth, was made tangible to the gross physical senses of mankind through a law well known to the mystic, and through which He manifested Himself to His disciples after His crucifixion. It is evident enough He was clothed upon with a spiritual form after being laid in the sepulchre. His objective body had a mission to the planet and man; in one way it acted as an anchor, in another as a healing leaven. He was the master of all secret forces, and through the concentration of the divine ray (which many are now coming to comprehend) His body was dissolved and became the property of the cosmic life of the planet.

Christ's Substance operated upon the cosmic life somewhat after the manner of ordinary inoculation practiced in the medical schools. At least, one might by that illustration gain some idea of the process through which the healing life came into contact with the elements from which the objective life is evolved.

The whole divine plan was as orderly and natural, and as easily comprehended, as the replacing of a dislocated joint, or the introduction of vaccine into the human circulation. It is methodical and not at all marvelous or miraculous. Christ's body and blood was inoculated into the life of the world. It was the only manner in which the life-giving element could be brought into contact with the disturbed and diseased Substance of human life.

Everything in God's universe is done in an orderly manner. It has been said, and wisely enough, that "God geometrizes." He certainly never works outside of law, and we may understand His methods as we do those employed by man; for instance, those of Tesla in his scheme of putting our world in communication with other planets, and our own method of unraveling the mystery of the planetary universe through our system of telescopy.

This interpretation of Christ's mission reveals the meaning of that mystic lesson which He gave His disciples, as recorded by John:

"My Father gives you the true bread, for the bread of God is He which descends from heaven, and is giving life to the world.

"I have descended from heaven, not that I may do my will; but the will of Him who sent me.

"I am the bread of life * * * I am that living bread who has descended from heaven; if any one eat of this bread, he shall live forever; and the bread is my flesh which I give for the life of the world.

"He who eats my flesh and drinks my blood, has eternal life. For my flesh is the true food, and my blood is the true drink.

"He who eats my flesh, and drinks my blood, abides in me, and I in him.

"The bread that I give is my body, which I give for the life of the world."

His parable of the leaven is symbolic of the infusion of His life into the Substance of things. We understand that the kingdom of heaven, to which He so often alluded in His teachings, is that regenerate state in man where the dual nature has been restored through that healing life, the infusion of His blood and body into the life of mankind.

He says: "The kingdom of heaven resembles leaven, which a woman taking, mingled in three measures of meal till the whole was fermented." Nothing could have expressed the effect of Christ's Substance on the mass of cosmic life more simply and comprehensively than the lesson of the leaven, possessing in its small bulk such a wonderful capacity of expansion and growth, and the power to infuse itself throughout the mass until all becomes perfect.

Our Lord enlightened Paul in all this sacred mystery, although He had gone from sight. It was through visions and revelations that Paul came into the knowledge of Christ's real nature and mission to the world; of His immaculate birth, His dual life, the significance of His death, and the efficacy of His body and blood. Paul knew "many things not lawful for a man to tell," for at that time these deeper truths could not be comprehended by the generality of mankind. With deep reverence and humility he declares: "To me, the very lowest of all saints, was this favor given to announce among the nations the glad tidings, even to enlighten all, as to what is the administration of that secret which has been concealed from the ages by that God who created all things."

There is nothing marvelous or needs be mysterious in this entire sacred drama, nothing outside of human possibilities. Christ is in all things our Teacher and Guide, and He has promised: "He that believeth on Me, the works that I do he shall do also; and greater works than these shall he do."

Although Christ gave Himself for the redemption of all things, yet man individually has a work to perform in the scheme. He must place himself in rapport with the saving principle. He can no more be saved without effort on his part than could a drowning man who refused to lay hold of the cable thrown out to him.

Man must cleanse his nature, change his line of thought, open his life to the inflowing of the divine healing principle which cannot permeate the animal plane; he must elevate his whole nature. He must not only redeem himself, but must help to redeem the lower kingdoms. "Indeed the earnest expectation of creation longs for the revelation of the 'Sons of God.'"

Who then are these "Sons of God?" They are the redeemed of the race, whenever and wherever they may be found; all of you here who have come into correct thinking and living.

"Whosoever will attain to divine contemplation, must mortify the anti-Christ in his soul, and depart from all own-hood of the will.   *   *   Through imagination, and an earnest, serious desire, we become again impregnated of the Deity, and receive the new body in the old."

—Jacob Boehme.

Benares, California, June 9th.

This morning, at the close of chapel services, Father Hyacinth announced that a large party of Knights Templar from San Francisco were to spend the day with us, dining at the Home and inspecting the institution generally.

This, of course, aroused the interest of the transient members of the family; for as sly as we may keep it, we all like a little smack of the outside world, however wicked it may be. Annie goes down to the junction almost every day, just to smell the wheel grease, she says, but I notice she manages to be on the spot only when the great express trains thunder in.

An extra train on our road will run down to the junction to meet the nine o'clock express from the west bringing in the Sir Knights, and Brother Paul has invited our party to go down with him and see them come in. The principal attraction for me this morning is the company of Brothers and Sisters, over two hundred in number, who will go down on our train as far as the orange orchards, there to stay over to gather fruit until the eleven o'clock train comes up, which will bring them to dinner, as every individual is expected to array himself or herself in his or her best in honor of the distinguished guests.

The fruit pickers were about equally divided as to men and women and old and young—if one could say old, regarding these people. Certain things they appear to have forgotten, such as getting wrinkled, sallow and peevish. I have a chronic distaste for crowds, and have always kept out of them if I could, until I came up here. Now I manage to get with the gatherings of these curious people whenever I can, they appear to rest me somehow, I cannot tell why, but they talk about unusual things, and talk low; and usually after I have been in Annie's company for a while I get so wrought up that if I can only fly out to the fields or orchards and just tag the "helpers," as they call them, from place to place, I become as serene and angelic as the best of them; and John says that he has hopes that I may be saved yet.

The honor of meeting and welcoming the guests had been given to Brother Eric—he being a member of the Order.

"You have no doubt been attracted toward Brother Eric in many ways," said Brother Paul, looking out under his heavy brows at John. "He has a history," he continued, "interesting beyond that of the generality of men." Then he fell into a thinking mood.

Brother Paul has a fascination about him that is most difficult to describe. He has a way of saying a few words, and then dropping off into a silence that expresses more than most people's words. So we sauntered along toward the train that stood snorting ready to start and was being filled with those who were going down to the orchards.

After we were seated, Brother Paul turned to us and said, "Brother Eric is master of ceremonies today, and I want you to watch him closely. His experience would fill a volume," he continued, "but he is so silent no one could read him from the surface; he is a man of deep and reverent nature and great dignity of character, in fact, a king among men. Later I will give you a short sketch of the past ten or twelve years of his life. He is so modest and retiring, that I fear you can never know his real nature or character; for self-sacrifice and good work he stands foremost in the ranks of the brotherhood."

At this point we arrived at the junction, just as the long express train began to move slowly out, looking like a huge reptile crawling over the face of the country. Standing upon the platform was a large party of distinguished looking and handsomely uniformed men; and as Brother Eric stepped forward to greet them, to my astonishment I saw that he too wore the dress of the Knights Templar. As he lifted his chapeau, saluting the company, I could not but admire his manly bearing, his broad shoulders, deep full chest; but above all, his magnificent head, like a great dome looming up. I have no words to express the air with which that man bore himself, as he advanced toward the company, each man uncovering his head to return the salutation. I turned and looked at John and Brother Paul, who both stood with uncovered heads. Annie for once in her life was silent, and I also, because I was afraid to speak, but I thought to myself, "Well, they have all caught it;" and I fell to thinking and studying and I have not found it out yet.

What a day that was! No language can express its fullness. I never had an opportunity to speak a word, but I just kept thinking. I recalled to mind that somewhere somebody had said that, "One day with the Lord was as a thousand years, and a thousand years as one day." I never could understand that kind of talk before.

After we were all seated at the dinner tables, Brother Eric rose and gave a brief but eloquent address welcoming the Sir Knights to the friendship of the brotherhood. How his face lighted up, and how lordly he did look. While he was speaking Annie leaned over and whispered in my ear, "That tow-headed Austrian is just too handsome for business," but she did not explain what business; it may have been some of her slang.

At the close of the banquet a fine stately gentleman—one of the Sir Knights—arose and gave a most flattering tribute to the colony and its workings, saying at the close of his speech that its foundation he believed was eternal, because of its principle of equal suffrage; that if any preference was shown at all it was given to the woman.

This, as a matter of course, brought forth prolonged applause, and if ever I was heartily glad that I was a woman it was on that occasion, to see the real deference that was shown the Sisters by those city men; but the beauty of the whole thing was that the Sisters commanded that respect, and those men could not help themselves. It was the most beautiful picture I ever saw; the Sisters in their graceful and classic dresses, the Brothers all in their white uniforms. The strange and unique sight evidently impressed those city-bred men deeply, from the fact that we fashionably and gaudily attired females presented not the slightest attraction for them.

But I didn't care; I was glad of it, for I knew that those women were beautiful, and that they were as good as they were beautiful. I knew that they possessed what women of the world can never know anything of; and I saw that these men of the world instinctively recognized in them a hidden but potent influence.

So that day passed, full of strange experiences to me, and the most deeply interesting of my life. But then my life is only a small one as yet.

Our visitors went down to meet the four o'clock express, having been deeply interested in what they had seen, judging from remarks made during the day. Brother Eric and Father Hyacinth accompanying the guests to see them off on their home-bound train.

Annie had arranged for a shorthand report of the day's proceedings for one of the Sir Knights, which he was to have published in the San Francisco dailies.

Brother Paul, John, Angela and myself started up the mountain for a little quiet chat before the evening gathering. After we had all been seated for some moments, drinking in the sublime beauty of the surrounding country, I began to wriggle about, I did not like the silence; then, too, I wanted to hear something about that man Eric.

Brother Paul has a queer manner of looking at people and never seeming to see them. What troubles me the most is the fact that these strange men and women talk more with their eyes than with their mouths; a kind of language that I have never gotten used to, although John and Angela use it generally, never appearing to require any words to help them in understanding each other perfectly. Silence may be a glorious thing, but talk is the average woman's birthright. Life is not of much consequence if she is deprived of that right.

I had endured this silence about as long as I could; I began to feel that I wanted to scream right out, or get up and run or kick or do something to break the spell, when Angela, in her quiet way, turning to Brother Paul, said, "I wish you would tell us something of Brother Eric's life; what you said of him this morning made him an object of double interest to us all I feel sure," looking at me as she finished speaking.

I looked up into Brother Paul's face. There was something in its expression that quieted my excitability in a few seconds, how or why I am sure I don't know; it is a power possessed by these confounded men. I hope to know some day how it is done.

"We never give utterance to any flattery, boasts or recrimination in this fraternity," said the Brother, quietly and slowly, without raising his eyes, "but if there was really expressed what is uppermost in each heart, it would be to say that Brother Eric stands, in all respects, as a member of this institution, trusted and loved beyond expression. He has permitted us to occasionally use his history as a lesson to those who believe in constitutional and irredeemable degradation." And with that he looked straight at me in a manner that made the cold chills creep up and down my back, so I never looked his way again, but I kept up a tremendous thinking.

"Eleven years ago this very month," he contlnned, "just at nightfall, there came to the Home a lone tramp of the most despicable type, judging from all appearances. Only those who have come into close relationship with tramp life can form any conception of what human life can sink into, of the degradation, of the worse than brute development. This man—if we could call him such—had evidently sounded the depths of all phases of crime of which tramp life is susceptible. But as we never refuse any applicants, or ask any questions, he was taken in and kindly attended to like all others.

"He did not utter a word for many days, until at length he was consulted as to what occupation he would prefer; he appeared then to brighten up, and at once chose bookkeeping, for which he has shown the utmost aptitude.

"At length he asked if he could be admitted into the brotherhood, which request was readily granted, for no one could then recognize in him the filthy, ragged, profane and degraded tramp of a few months previous. When he was initiated, he was asked what name he would prefer to go by. After a long and expressive silence, he said, 'You may call me Eric, but above all I wish you would call me Brother,' and tears, as only such men can shed, were rolling down his broad cheeks.

"No one ever questioned him as to his past life, but when he had been with us a year he was trusted with any and everything. He was such an accomplished accountant that he took charge of nearly all of the sales, our business never having been so well managed as through him. This is a collossal enterprise, this plantation of five thousand acres."

How the man's face lighted up as he progressed.

"You have noticed," he continued, turning to John, "that there are between twenty and thirty freight cars sent out daily loaded with oranges, and twice that number with grapes and other fruit; this part of the enterprise is under Eric's management.

"When he had been with us two years we had grown to worship the man, he exhibited so many grand traits; then, too, he was so modest, he stood out a kind of grand figurehead, and we would find ourselves quoting Eric on all occasions. It became to me alarming, although I never breathed my fears, still I knew too well the effect on all of hero-worship. From his entrance into the fraternity he had become a part of myself; we made no manifestation of regard, but each would have died for the other and counted it gain."

"A modern Damon and Pythias,'" suggested Angela, smiling.

"Yes, quite equal," answered the narrator,

laughing good humoredly; "I can smile now, but there was a time when I could not.

"To proceed, for it is near our supper hour. When Eric had been with us two years there came an unusual large and important order from San Francisco for small fruit, and it was deemed advisable for Eric to go there and superintend the matter personally. The train was enormous in size, and of great value, being of the early and perishable fruits. It was made up and despatched, and Eric was to telegraph us within twenty-four hours; as we very naturally felt anxious concerning the matter, it being a new venture, and rather an experiment in fact. So when twenty-four hours lapsed into thirty-six, and thirty-six into forty-eight, and yet no word or sign, we concluded that something must be wrong, so I started on after him. I traced the train into the freight sheds in San Francisco, and was told that the cars had been unloaded on their arrival. Then I began to reconnoiter the city. I found that the fruit had all been disposed of on its arrival at the highest price and in the most perfect order, but I could not find my man. I continued my search with the assistance of the best police force in the city for twenty-four hours without the shadow of a clue. I had then given up in despair and was about to return home, when I met on the street one of the freight agents whom I had previously talked with. He came up to me and said, 'I believe your man is in one of the cars, locked in; we can hear something in the car, but it is locked on the inside and we cannot get in, and would not force the door until we had seen you.'

"Well, we went down to the depot and forced the car door open; and there, sure enough, lay our Eric dead drunk. After he had finished his business he had locked himself up in the car with his jugs of liquor about him and became oblivious to everything else. If I had found him dead from an assassin's hand—had he but died in honor—I should have been happy in comparison to what I then suffered."

Then Paul had another spell, and we had to wait. At length he continued.

"Upon examining his person I found all the money safely folded in his belt and strapped about him, showing that he had completed perfectly all his business before touching the liquor.

"He was utterly unconscious of anything, so I arranged a good comfortable bed, and with the help of one of the men put him in it. I threw away the intoxicants, secured some wholesome food, had our train run out and attached to one going east, then took up my station beside the poor fellow, and by daylight the next morning we found ourselves switched off on a side track at Benares.

"I can never forget the look in that man's eyes when he came to consciousness and realized what had transpired. He appeared to sense all that had taken place after he had lost his consciousness. He had done the thing, of all others, that he would not had he kept his equilibrium. I could feel that strong man's agony, and would have given my life to have relieved him. I asked no questions; I only held his hands in mine, and silently prayed for help.

"You know what all such things mean," said Paul, looking around squarely at John.

I knew only too well that John had been through many such scenes, and now his tender eyes were filled with tears.

"After a time," continued Brother Paul, "Eric controlled himself sufficiently to speak to me. 'I think it wisest that I should not go back to the Home,' he said in a low disconsolate voice. 'If you could but know what I have suffered! Drink has been my curse from the first. O God, have mercy upon me! I will not disgrace you, dearest and most patient friend.' He was covering my hands with kisses and his burning tears, rising he unbuckled the belt from around his body, and handing it to me, said, 'There is the money for the sales, all safe; it was one of the most profitable ever made, and oh! if I could only have been man enough to have resisted that accursed appetite,' and he fell prone upon the floor of the car and shook as only such men shake in their grief.

"After he had quieted down a little I said to him, 'Eric, you must go back to the Home; no one will ever know that anything has happened; you can go right on with your work; I know that such an accident will never happen again.' I took him in my arms and held him close to my heart and asked the Master to stay by us both; I bathed his swollen and tear-stained face, combed his disheveled hair and brushed his clothing, constantly speaking words of encouragement. The cars having been side-tracked, no one knew that we had returned, so I felt that I could take my time and straighten the fellow up. He sobbed and trembled like a child who had been fearfully beaten, never once looking into my face.

"After I had brushed him up, and infused a

kind of new life into him, he looked up into my face and said, 'My disgrace must not be concealed from the fraternity; I cannot live under false colors; they must know it all. I can trust them. They will help me, if I am worthy.'

"I wish," Brother Paul resumed, after a slight pause, "that I could describe to you the peculiar expression in that man's eyes when he at last looked me full in the face. There was the impress of a fearful experience, and a resolve; an expression that has never departed nor ever will. At his request a meeting of the fraternity was called, that meeting is as a sealed book, but it is registered in heaven.

"That all happened over nine years ago. Eric has gone regularly, and alone, every year to the large cities arranging for the marketing of our fruit, nothing has ever occurred since; we have had no more anxiety concerning him than we have of Sister Irene when she goes to the city to arrange for the shipping of her honey," looking over toward me and smiling, because he knew that Sister Irene was my patron saint.

"It seems sad though that he should have been so humiliated before the fraternity. Could it not just as well have been kept from them?" Angela asked in a low voice.

" 'There is a divinity that shapes our ends, rough hew them how we may,' " repeated Brother Paul slowly. "We were all growing to make an idol of him; he had need to fall in order to show us our error. We must not worship Personality. It is true that he is now often given the place of honor because he has shown himself a prince among men, has become master of himself. In early life, before he fell, he stood high in the Masonic fraternity, and was perfectly at home with those men who were here today."

At this juncture the supper bell rang and we all walked off silently toward the Home, no one uttering a word on the way. But I kept up a thinking; I recalled the fact that John had always said that Good was the only cure for Evil; and I remembered how I had battled with him for what I declared was sheer nonsense, maintaining that the world would never be any better unless people were punished severely for their evil doings.

As we came up to the porch we met Father Hyacinth and Brother Eric just returning from the junction. How grand that Norseman looked, calm, quiet and self-possessed.

Can such things be? And did he descend into the dregs? I ask myself, as this grand dignified man passed on in advance of us. Alas! how little we know of the reality of life, and the things that go to make up life.

"To him that overcometh will I give of the hidden manna (i. e., essential bread), and I will give him a white stone (i. e., an incorruptible body), and upon the stone a new word (i. e., title) written, which no man knoweth but he that receiveth it."

—Revelation ii. 17.

CHAPTER VII.

Benares, California, June 16th.

This morning, after breakfast, the Westlake family, John, Annie and myself, started out on a reconnoitering expedition up the side of the mountain. After a time we came to a deep ravine, along the side of which there was a well-beaten roadway that appeared to have been much traveled. We could none of us understand its use away up there, almost beyond the timber line. We strolled on, it appeared to me a full mile, some of the way quite steep, when presently we came in sight of a large singularly shaped stone building, nearly completed, a number of workmen still engaged upon it.

As we neared the building, one of the Brothers, who seemed to be inspecting the work, came forward, and John enquired of him the nature of the edifice.

"This is our Observatory," he answered; "we

are quite anxious to get it completed as our telescope is to be here next week."

This was all so new to us that we were silent for some moments, when John said, "I was not aware that you were building an Observatory. How long have you been on the work?"

"We commenced the building three years ago," he answered; "it has necessarily progressed slowly because we work only a given number of hours each day—not more than five or six. Then nearly all of our material is taken in the rough, right up here; we burn our own lime for our mortar; the stone for our walls and the slate for roofing comes from the quarries right here; we get our wood from lower down the mountain; we make our own putty. The glass, nails and iron trimmings are about all that we import. Our progress is rather slow, but everything is done upon honor; we have, as a matter of course, a large force of 'Helpers.' "

"What is to be the calibre of your instrument?" asked Sir Anthony Westlake.

"It is to be equal in every respect, if not superior, to the one in the Lick Observatory. You must examine our building; there is not another in the country as fine in finish and appointments."

We entered and inspected the structure, which Sir Charles considered quite equal to that of Sir Francis Galtons in England.

"Who was your architect?" he asked of the Brother.

"Brother Paul drew up the plan," replied the man; "he is quite an astronomer, and has visited all of the observatories of any note, both in Europe and in this country, and has improved upon them all we think," smiling good naturedly.

"Do you have no overseer or superintendent from the outside world?" asked the Englishman.

"No," replied the Brother. "Every man is his own overseer and superintendent. Every one of the twenty-five men at work here is equally capable of following out Brother Paul's plans, each man endeavors to see how perfectly he can perform the work allotted to him. We all have an especial pride in this building; every member of the fraternity is full of anticipation concerning this additional facility for study and research."

"Well, this colony I consider one of the marvels of this century," said Sir Charles Westlake as we were descending the mountain. "Had the plan been presented to me before coming here I should have pronounced it entirely utopian, but their resources are marvelous, considering where they are. I examined their library, and was astonished not only at the quantity but also at the quality of the reading matter it contained. They appear not only to be all artists and artisans, but scholars as well," he said, laughing.

"They do not permit you to call them 'workmen,'" I said, remembering what Sister Alicia had said to me; "they are 'Helpers.'"

"Well," he said, laughing heartily, "whatever they call themselves, they are a really wonderful people."

Annie now monopolized the attention of the young lord, and fell back on the pretense of getting some ferns and flowers that grew in an inaccessible place, and which she sent his lordship clambering over rocks and brambles to gather. She had that faculty which so many girls have, of always appropriating in a company what they consider the "catch" of the occasion.

I don't mention this from any feeling of jealousy, for I did not want the English lord's attention, for I would rather have John's little finger than all the lords in creation.

The rest of our party strolled on down toward Home, as it was now nearly time for the lesson.

A Brother walking down with us remarked on the way that in two weeks there was to be an excursion party from Los Angeles, which would be quite an interesting affair, as the party was to remain over night and visit the Observatory, the telescope would then be in working order. The visitors had been invited by the Brothers in honor of the occasion.

"I would like to enquire where you people get all the means for procuring these luxuries; the elegant buildings, furniture, telescopes, etc?" asked Sir Anthony Westlake. "In my country it requires money, a vast deal of it, even to live quietly, and here you have luxuries and an abundance of them."

"Our institution is now self-sustaining," answered the Brother. "Our income far exceeds our outlay. We have five thousand acres of land, a large portion of it under a high state of cultivation. We have at this time six hundred acres of the choicest variety of grapes just ready for the market. A large part of the labor is performed by the fraternity, except in extreme cases, as in the gathering of fruits that ripen simultaneously, like grapes, when we are obliged to import our help by the hundreds." Here smiling and waving an adieu he turned off into another path and we continued on.

"As far as I have been able to judge, they all appear well educated," said Sir Anthony.

"This is really a school," John replied; "they have every facility for education. I have rarely been in colleges that were better equipped than their school rooms. Those who enter the institution from time to time, who have had no opportunities in early life, go through a course of primary studies, and after a time through the more advanced course. There is no place in this colony for ignorance, lack of discipline or lack of self-control."

"So I see," said the Englishman, apparently in a brown study, walking slowly with his head down and his hands clasped behind him.

We had now reached the Home, and saw the guests from without all going toward the chapel, and heard the grand old clock chiming the quarter to nine.

John drew my arm through his, saying in a low voice, "You must listen carefully to the lesson this morning, for it is a deeply significant subject and I would like you to understand the full meaning of all of these teachings."

"I will try," I answered seriously, "for your sake."

After we had been seated a few moments Annie entered, smiling radiantly, followed by her young lord with his arms full of brush, looking foolish and disgusted. I glanced slyly up at John's face, and saw a merry twinkle in his honest brown eyes, and the dimples deepen in his cheeks; the Boston man, leaning his head down on the back of John's seat, fairly shook with suppressed laughter. They all enjoyed Annie's little harmless maneuvering at times.

"And for this cause, Man above all things that live upon Earth, is double; mortal, because of his Body, and immortal because of the substantial Man.

"And being Hermaphrodite, or Male and Female, and watchful, he is governed by, and subjected to a Father, that is both Male and Female, and watchful."

—Hermes, in "Divine Pymander."

"Increased practice of celibacy is the only means for any real advancement of the race; the celibacy which is not the result of restraint, but the outcome of a spiritual growth, producing deep conviction and general elevation of character.

The commonest objection taken against celibacy is that if practiced by all it will bring the world to an end. This line of argument entirely ignores the dynamic power of thought, which the celibates will bring to bear upon those desirous of issue; and thus the general average of humanity, far from deteriorating, will be likely to improve."

—Fragments of Forgotten History.

SEVENTH LESSON.

CELIBACY.

"The children of this age marry and are given in marriage; but those that are deemed worthy to attain to the kingdom and the resurrection from the dead, neither marry or are given in marriage. For in those days, those before the Deluge, they were eating and drinking, marrying and pledging in marriage, till the day that Noah entered the ark, and understood not till the Deluge came and swept them all away."

"And they sang as it were a new song. * * * And no one was able to learn that song except the hundred and forty-four thousand, those who were redeemed from the earth. These are those who were not defiled with women, for they were virgins. These were redeemed from men."

We have every assurance that the race was created androgynous or double, each individual possessing both the male and female characteristics; that it was angelic, knowing nothing of what we call sin. Now as Man was created in the image of God, we come to the conclusion that like his Creator he must be changeless and deathless; so that whatever may present itself to us in our investigation in this direction we can always fall back on that fact.

The double angelic individual, possessing within his or herself the divine mate—the two in one—is a being altogether beyond our present comprehension, but we believe in it all the same. In our sacred annals we learn that as long as Man preserved his androgynous character and attended strictly to the business assigned to him, he was not only righteous but was perfectly happy also.

We have discovered in our study that Man, somewhere along his journey, cultivated a disposition to pry into things, and as he required suitable implements with which to work, he invented a species of home-made law, quite outside of and unknown to divine jurisdiction; he also tinkered up some kind of a machine that he called "mind" to match it; and in time fell to thinking on a very curious plane of thought that changed his whole being, mentally, morally and physically, so that he was apparently no longer one whole, all round and perfect being, but there were two very inferior halves; and sometimes not quite halves—a fact that we are being constantly made aware of.

Then later on we hear of the "fall of Man," that greatest of all catastrophes in the world's history—or so we judge. We learn also that the cause of the "fall" of Man was his losing sight of his divine helpmate within, and his starting on a race for something or someone outside of himself; thereby, according to our best authorities, committing a species of adultery by his transgression of the law of wholeness. The punishment for which was the development on our earth of every form of sin, sickness, discord and death; as we have been previously informed.

Now from the heights, after contemplating those angelic beings created in the image of God, we will descend and make the acquaintance of the nineteenth century individual; who, after countless ages of mismanagement in doing business on his own responsibility, is beginning to realize that there is a screw loose in the machinery somewhere. He is coming into a consciousness — somewhat dimly perhaps — that there is something in existence beside himself. There are times when, back of all the jar, discord, confusion and mistakes, he feels half consciously the steady push of infinite design.

Many things that man through his mis-step has been forced to do in the old regime, are no longer admissible in this our new dispensation. A misdemeanor in a child would be overlooked because of ignorance; but in one matured and knowing the law, a transgression would be considered a sin, and punishable as such. "If I had not spoken unto them, they would not have had sin, but now they have no excuse for their sins," said the Master.

To the more advanced of the human race, celibacy has become an imperative law, the transgression of which brings to the individual indescribable suffering, and in a degree degradation in various forms.

The Indian proverb says, "He who desires offspring desires death, the immortal must be celibate.

"The married relation, which accentuates the difference between man and woman, is utterly incompatible with the higher life.

"Adeptship is the peculiar heritage of the celibate.

"The spiritual wisdom of the world has been the offspring of the celibate."*

* Fragments of Forgotten History.

The robust health and fine physical development usually existing among Catholic priests is the result of the celibate life. All people who have lived strictly and conscientiously up to this life escape the ordinary diseases that attack the generality of mankind. In monastic institutions, where there are at times hundreds of inmates, living often in close quarters, there are rarely, if ever, cases of sickness of such character as ordinarily prevail among the pupils of schools and colleges.

This fact is easily accounted for, when we understand that celibacy is the foundation upon which all such institutions are founded, and is conscientiously practiced by its devotees. To live in obedience to the law of chastity must influence for good the entire life of the individual, physically, morally and mentally.

When we fully realize that the real Man is still dual, and that the division is only in the perishable animal man and no more enduring, it will be plain enough to the individual that he can easily outgrow that low habit of thought, just as readily as he denies away many other criminal suggestions of his mind of the flesh. This change cannot take place in the individual without some effort or preparation on his part.

He will need to think deeply and upon religious and spiritual subjects, dwelling long and earnestly; until, like Milton, he can see with spiritual eyes.

"Till oft converse with heavenly habitants
 Begin to cast a beam on the outward shape,
 The unpolluted temple of the Mind,
 And turns it by degrees to the soul's essence,
 Till all be made immortal."

Christ was an example of the regenerate Man; the recovered Man; and the race is to attain to His state. He came to demonstrate the law of celibacy—to restore that lost art. His advent on this planet was not a miracle, but a demonstration of the law of chastity. Celibacy was the core of His teachings, and that of all those disciples who were prepared to understand His more occult lessons. He said to His faithful few, "To you it is given to know the mysteries of God's kingdom, but to others in parables only." But even in his more external teachings there is ample proof of His doctrine of celibacy. He said, "The children of this age marry and are given in marriage, but those deemed worthy to obtain that world, and that resurrection from the dead, neither marry nor are given in marriage, because they are like angels, and are sons of God, being sons of the resurrection." "And the disciples say to Him, It is not good to marry?" "He answered, None can admit the word (the teaching) but those to whom it is given; for there are some eunuchs by natural constitution, others have been made eunuchs by men, and others have made themselves eunuchs on the account of the kingdom of the heavens. He who is able to do this let him do it."

The term "eunuch," as ordinarily employed, has not the same significance as in the teaching of Christ. The translators have used the word eunuch for the want of a more appropriate term for those of whom He was speaking. In one case He declares that the individual had been born above the carnal law, that is, of a dual nature; "For there are some eunuchs by natural constitution." In another instance there had been evolved through religious thought and purity of life in the person, that at-onement of the two natures; "Such have made themselves eunuchs on the account of the 'kingdom of the heavens.'" In brief, they have received the Holy Spirit. "Others have been made eunuchs by men." Have been made eunuchs through the manual process known at the present time as asexualization.

Paul in his more mystical teaching says, "I wish all men to be even as myself, * * * the time being shortened; it remains that those having wives should be as not having them.

"You who formerly were afar off, are made near by the blood of Christ. * * * Having by His flesh annulled the law" (that is the carnal or sex law).

"That He might form the two in Himself unto one new man. * * * * Who will transform the body of our humiliation unto conformity with His glorious body."

By which we understand that through the divine Substance of Christ we are to be healed of that race-mark of sin, and that there is to be an awakening in man of the divine dual consciousness; a blossoming out of the Christlikeness within him, as Paul saw it. "He will transform the body of our humiliation (that which was our humiliation) into conformity with His glorious body."

Jacob Boehme expresses it: "Through imagination, and in earnest serious desire, we become again impregnated of the Deity, and receive the new body in the old." We must be "born again"

—to use a hackneyed expression—must be regenerated.

An important crisis occurs in the evolution of the psychic nature in every individual. A culminating point in the growth toward that change known as regeneration or the "new birth." It is the scene of the "temptation," an experience that none can escape. If at this point in his growth the individual descends to the animal plane, hoping to live in both worlds at the same time, he will, if he continues to occupy this debatable ground, not only suffer mental and physical torture, but open the doors to the most unholy of influences, "And the last state of that man will be worse than the first."

There are many in these latter days who are on that debatable ground, who long to be emancipated; yet who know nothing of those laws that control their spiritual nature. The sufferings of such are indescribable. These are their birth throes, and they do not know where to look for deliverance.

To the lover of his kind, there are presented at this time many distressing and discouraging features in the management of human affairs. It is not alone the eye of the pessimist that detects these portends of coming calamity; but the philanthropist, the humanitarian, and even the altruist, looks on with forebodings.

The race has been so long under the dominion of the animal sex law that there has been bred in the physical constitution a deadly disease, a plague spot, contagious and destructive in its effects, not only on the physical lives of men and women, but damning to the soul as well. This disease does not exist alone in the unmentionable abodes of sin, or in the low dens of crime; but prevails alike in high places, regardless of position, culture or education. It has become a race malady. Forty years' practice as a physician among women has convinced me that the prevalence of those affections peculiar to females is caused wholly from the transgression of the law controlling the dual life. This sin against the divine law is the cause of the constantly increasing nervous derangements and insanity, which so far have baffled the skill of the most learned of the medical fraternity. The divided sex poison becomes, to both men and women, under certain conditions destructive in its effect upon the brain and nerve centers, inducing nervous diseases which are incurable without a life of total abstinence from the exciting cause.

The reason for the effect of this transgression

being so much more destructive to woman than to man is because the female side of humanity has never yet wholly lost the image of the divine feminine—"the dual type;" they have not yet come totally under the law of degeneracy, and are therefore many degrees higher and nearer redemption than the masculine. That is why woman suffers so keenly from the prevailing wrongs. The nearer a soul is to its regeneration, the more does it suffer from the commission of sin.

To live a celibate life not only tends to heal and elevate the individual, but to influence for good all other lives with whom he or she may come in intimate contact. The overcoming of this animal instinct will be the soul's Gethsemane. It is the door opening into that kingdom of God which is within you all.

One having overcome the animal nature has no longer any desire for the ownership, monopoly or possession of an individual life. Such no longer speak of "my wife," "my husband" or "my children," but instead "our brother," "our sister," "our friend," "our Father!" from whom the whole family in the heavens and on earth is named. Among the animal qualities overcome will be his "myness."

This change in the life will not narrow the sympathies and render one selfish, but, instead, will broaden and deepen the whole nature. It will have annihilated the animal selfhood in man and woman, rendering them capable of loving their neighbor as themselves.

Here arises a somewhat exciting and weighty question: If celibacy becomes a general practice, how is the world to become populated? you ask.

This is a difficult question to answer. We can only fall back on the statement that forms the principal support of our theory. That God having made man androgynous—in His own likeness and after His own image—the androgynous man is therefore really a fixed fact in creation, only requiring recognition to become an established order. Then according to the wise ordering of things, which we are too corrupt to comprehend at present, immaculate conception would be again established; there being nothing mysterious or marvelous in it, Mary and Jesus being our open examples.

Celibacy cannot in this age become a prevailing practice, from the fact that the teaching cannot be accepted but by the few who have reached that climacteric stage in their experience which demands a radical change in their physical mode of living; there need be no fear so far as the "end of the world" is concerned. Christ said, "He that is able to receive it, let him receive it." There will be, no doubt, some little time yet before celibacy will become universal. I fear it will not be in our time.

There is little danger of any lack of population; the greater weight of the world's sorrow is caused by the surplus of a certain grade of human life that is constantly increasing in volume.

According to Boehme, "The end of the world," which has been so long the terror of the average of mankind, is simply the end of animal generation.

To the true lover of mankind, the Christian, humanitarian and philanthropist, the most deeply interesting problem of the hour is—or should be—the mental, moral and physical condition of those most largely engaged in propagating the human species. Who is it that is filling our foundling hospitals, homes for the feeble minded, houses of correction, houses of illfame, reform schools, work houses, prisons, and many other institutions established for the alleviation of evils from over-production of certain grades of human beings?

The majority of the population of the world at this time live but a little above the animal plane; a proportion sinking even below the brute in degradation, being usually the more prolific; while the mentally, morally and physically well balanced portion of the race add but a limited number to the advanced types in these days. A large proportion of the refined, cultured and well-to-do people enter into the marriage relation with a fixed intention of avoiding offspring. Taking it altogether the replenishing of the human family is left mainly to those wholly unfit for the parental office.

Now the vital and all-absorbing question of the hour is not, How shall we increase the population of the world? but, rather, How shall we stay the tide of the over-production of the deformed, imbecile, degraded and vicious humanity that is hourly being multiplied?

There appears to be one solution to the matter; it is, that inasmuch as man established the law of animal generation, it devolves upon him to regulate the working of that law, especially the law of fecundity, that generally governs in the lower orders. We understand that the propagation of the carnal man is outside of the divine law, "For it is not subject to the law of God, neither indeed can it be," Paul informed us.

There must be something done in the line of human effort, quite different from anything that has yet been attempted, to regulate the sex relations, especially in the depraved, diseased, deformed, imbecile and criminal ranks, to prevent an increase along that line of the low grade of human life.

We can see a way to a better state of things; can see a solution to this mighty problem. It is Asexualization! That, and that alone, will regulate the stupendous wrongs that now curse the race. If asexualization became an established law for the regulation of the unfortunate, as it should, a few generations would produce a marked change upon the race; as the propagation of the species would be left to those who regard the parental office as something sacred, and who would impress upon their progeny the nobler and purer qualities; and in time there would be developed a grand race of men and women, each generation approaching more nearly to the perfect state of "two in one."

The reconstructed race will not be composed, as today, of men and women of widely divided and erratic natures, constantly at variance and at war with each other; but a family of divinely symmetrical beings, grandly balanced, possessing all noble and sweet qualities, as well as the power to understand God's works and the capacity to perform them as well. By degrees the original order of things will be restored, and gradually immaculate conception will become the law. Whatever has been done through divine law, will be again done; it is a law that can never be broken. There will be more Marys and more immaculate conceptions.

God will again establish His laws upon the earth. We cannot tell where or when this may be manifested, but we know that He never fails, and we have His promise. Our Lord, when asked when the kingdom of God should come, said, "When two shall be as one, and that which is without as that which is within."

There was a period in the history of the planet when the same questions agitated the minds of men as today. What shall we do with our waste population? And when is the world coming to an end?

"They did eat, they drank, they married wives, they were given in marriage, until the day that Noah entered into the ark, and the flood came, and destroyed them all. And as it was in the days of Noah, so shall it be also in the days of the Son of man.".

That episode in human history known as the Deluge was the result of the degradation of mankind at that period; and because of the oneness of all things, our poor tortured planet collapsed, lost its balance, tipped over on one side, thereby washing away large portions of the race, Noah and his family being among the saved. We read also that Noah was a "just man, and perfect in his generations, and Noah walked with God;" so he must have been superior to the man of today. And Noah had three sons; we do not read of any daughters; and according to our authority Noah lived nine hundred and fifty years —a long time.

It is evident that Noah and his sons—as these beings are called—were androgynous or hermaphroditic, having preserved through all pestilence and corruption their dual nature. "Noah was a just man, and perfect in his generations." The androgynous being could never have known sickness or pain, as both of these are outgrowths of sexual life—poison. Therefore it need not be condemned as a myth, the story of Noah's advanced age.

We have learned that during the first era God blessed the race and bade them to be fruitful, "And God saw everything that He had made, and behold it was very good. And the Lord God walked among men."

Then the third era dawned, and man had developed the power of producing the animal man, as we learn. But this method of populating the world was not blessed as in the case of the original. The Lord did not pronounce it "good," but as we have seen frowned upon it. "Unto the woman he said, I will greatly multiply thy sorrows and thy conceptions; in sorrow shalt thou bring forth."

Why bring forth in sorrow? One of the most troublesome, puzzling and harrassing questions of the day is that of the sex relations and the office of maternity. Have you never, in pondering over this subject, queried as to the wisdom of the whole matter? Wondering why the subject should be clothed upon with dishonor, secrecy and shame. Things never to be spoken of openly, as are all other inevitable states and circumstances in life. Why should this be as it is? If God ordained these things, then they must be all right, wise and honorable. Why clothe them with shame? Do we need to crimson over God's work?

But if He did not order them, then what? "I will greatly multiply thy sorrows. In sorrow thou shalt bring forth." Why shall she bring forth in sorrow? God had pronounced all of His work good; why condemn this, which appears to us to be rather an important affair?

This is the explanation. Animal generation was the mark of that sin which the race committed. It was the brand of man's disobedience; in fact it was a curse: "I will greatly multiply thy sorrows." Here is the reason why the sex and maternal functions are spoken of in secret and with bated breath and shame-faced glances. It is because the divine instinct in the spiritual Man recoils at the perversion of what was, in the original and angelic family, the highest and holiest office, that of Motherhood!

"For the Woman is the crown of Man, and the final manifestation of humanity. * * * She is nearest to the throne of God, when she shall be revealed."

So that women shall no more lament their womanhood; but men shall rather say, "Oh, that we had been born women!"

"And her reign shall be greater than the reign of the Man; * * * * and she shall have dominion forever."

"And she that is alone shall bring forth more children to God than she who hath a husband. But the creation of the woman is not yet complete; but it shall be complete in the time which is at hand."

—Perfect Way.

Benares, California, June 20th.

As we dispersed this morning, after the usual services, each following his or her own inclination or call to duty, I observed that the handsome guest car with a steaming engine stood at the entrance of the grounds, ready to run down to the junction for some purpose unknown to the majority of us. Nothing had been said either at breakfast or in chapel concerning any new movement, consequently there was much questioning and speculations among the members of the class. I, being true to my American instinct, a desire to know other people's business, began to look for someone who could give the desired information concerning the matter.

As I strolled down toward the train, I saw John in close conversation with Brother Eric, who, as I approached, walked off toward the car and boarded it. He was clad in the full costume of the Order and carried himself like a prince as usual.

As John came up and drew my arm through his, he said, as we walked slowly back toward the Home, "We are to be honored by a stunning event today, which we worldlings know nothing of, because these people do not talk about their affairs very much in advance, and thus, I fancy, have deeper enjoyment than we do, who spread everything out, diluting it by much talking over it before it really happens."

"Well, never mind about that," I said pettishly; "what is going to happen? let's have it."

John eyed me keenly for a moment, without uttering a word, and I am always willing to keep still and wait when he looks that way. At length he said, "A party is to visit the colony this morning composed of the wealthy and privileged classes, great railroad magnates, many times millionaires, having their own train, their French chef, family physician, maids, nurses, waiters, etc.; in fact, every luxury that money can procure."

"How in the world did they ever happen to come here?" I asked in open-eyed wonder.

John answered, "The leading man of the expedition, it appears, at one time knew Brother Eric intimately, and because of some unaccountable personal attraction has felt inclined to keep trace of the Brother all these years, and latterly has written to him expressing a strong desire to visit the colony, and as the excursion party would pass the junction en route for San Francisco, the temptation was too great for this friend of earlier years to resist. An invitation of the most cordial nature from the leading members of the Brotherhood was at once extended to the travelers. A committee has been appointed to perfect all arrangements at the junction. The train will be switched off, thus permitting the guests time to inspect the institution. Eric has gone down to welcome them and bring them up to the Home. They are not far distant from the sound of that whistle," added my companion, turning his smiling face in the direction of the sound.

At this juncture, Annie joined us, all of a flutter. "Only think of it, John," she cried, clutching his disengaged arm, "a company of real millionaires are coming in their own palace car! I am going to dress in my very best for the occasion." And away she flew up to her dormitory, from which she descended in a few minutes looking as serene and sweet as an angel, a faculty that she pre-eminently possessed.

A large group composed of the family and students had seated themselves on the lawn and Brother Paul was giving them a little object lesson in chemistry, "Solidified Air," I guess; that man knows all about such things.

After he had completed his experiment and

put aside his chemicals, he said, "We will just keep our seats out here, and watch the proceedings, and be ready for any development."

Then we all fell into a silence; that is the best way I can express it, and Brother Paul "looked into futurity." That is what Annie calls those periods of silence, that no one would dare to break any more than they would dare to scream out in meeting.

Presently Annie pressed close to me and whispered, "What a world of mystery surrounds this people, and yet how fascinating, how different from that world and that people that we have always known. Where and how will it all end?"

Off in the distance we can hear the powerful engine puffing and wheezing, toiling up the hill with its precious burden of human life.

The great clock struck the hour of nine, and Brother Paul said, breaking the silence, "We shall not have the pleasure of dining with the distinguished guests, as many of you doubtless have hoped to do," looking up under his brows at Annie.

"May I enquire why we are not?" cried Annie, getting very red in the face, and sitting up straight. "I was informed," she continued, "that the party was to dine at the Home, and that Brother Eric had made special arrangements to that effect." She squared herself around facing Brother Paul, looking defiant and disturbed.

" 'The best laid plans o' mice and men gang aft aglee,' " muttered the mystic; then, turning toward the excited girl, he said, "The leading man, it appears, declined Eric's invitation for the party to dine with us when he learned that we served neither wines nor meat at our board, remarking that the company would just take a little look at the place— 'the town,' as he called it—and return to their car for dinner; remarking, by way of explanation and apology, that the members of the company were all high livers and could never take a dinner without their wine, and as their supplies were all so abundant he thought they had better dine on the car. Almost anyone but Brother Eric would have felt chagrined at the refusal, but nothing moves him, not even the fact that he was not invited to dine with his old-time friend on the palace car," and Brother Paul laughed heartily, exclaiming at the same time, "But here comes our Brother and his honored guests."

Annie sprang from her seat, flushed and excited, and before we could think or speak she was half way across the lawn on her way to be presented to the visitors.

There were about twenty in all, but only three of the ladies had cared to visit the Home, each accompanied by her maid carrying fans, sunshades, wraps and salts; the remainder of the party not having interest enough in the "barbarians," as they styled the members of the brotherhood, to expose themselves to the heat in order to see them.

Brother Frederick, being on the committee to arrange for the comfort of the guests at the junction, doubtless heard many things not intended for the ears of the fraternity.

Sister Alicia, assisted by Annie, who was in an ecstasy of delight, was arranging easy chairs and rugs on the cool and capacious porches for the ladies and their maids, the ladies declining seats on the lawn for fear of bugs and worms.

The gentlemen manifested deep interest in the town, in the fine architecture and the superior quality of granite used in the buildings; but what appeared to astonish them most was the extent of the territory owned by the brotherhood, and all of which was under such a perfect state of cultivation.

At the close of their tour of inspection they

came around where our party was seated, and the first question asked by the speaker on the occasion was, "Where does all the money come from? for you have here not merely every comfort, but absolute elegance."

Brother Paul explained in a few concise words, and then, to the astonishment of all present, stated the amount of funds in the repository at the present time.

"Well! what do you intend to do with your surplus means?" bluntly asked one of the visitors, a large man, walking up beside Brother Paul.

What a contrast between the two men! The stranger was evidently about the same age as the Brother, and had doubtless been of equally fine proportions, but he was now excessively stout and flushed and breathing with great difficulty.

A smile broke over the face of the mystic, as he arose and stood beside the man of the world, displaying in contrast his finely developed chest, clear cut features and brilliant eyes.

"We have great need for money at all times," he said, gently and courteously, "not merely for the purpose of establishing new colonies in various portions of the country, but to assist the poor and oppressed wherever found; to aid the

Labor Unions in their struggles in cases of strikes, not alone in this country but in foreign lands also."

"It is barely possible that you are attending to that which is really none of your affairs," interposed one of the gentlemen, his face flushed and his eyes sparkling with excitement.

"Oh, no, we think not," replied the Brother, smilingly. "Wherever there is suffering in any form we consider it our affairs to do what we can to alleviate it. The interest of the human family is all one with us."

"What use do you make of all these immense buildings? you have a city up here," smilingly questioned one of the ladies who had ventured out and joined our group.

Brother Eric turned to the fair visitor and said gravely, "We have here our institutions of learning, our libraries, our repositories and our hospitals. Here we receive the most degraded tramps and criminals that the world has produced, and they are treated and healed with as much certainty as we would treat and heal fever patients. You will understand that it requires a large amount of money to successfully operate such a school, reformatory and hospital as we have here."

"Where are all your tramps and criminals?" asked a spruce looking young man, with a slight curl of the lip.

"We haven't any," replied the Brother, turning his handsome smiling face toward his questioner. "When they come to us they cease to be tramps and criminals, and become students and law abiding citizens of our Social Democracy."

The first speaker fanned himself vigorously with his hat, looking first at Brother Paul, then at Brother Eric, in blank amazement, then said impatiently, "You will see what all your Socialistic ideas will amount to; they will only stir up strife and cause strikes."

"That is just what we desire," interposed Brother Eric, in a tone of voice that made the chills creep over me.

How that man can expand in all directions when he gets aroused. What a model he would have made for the Colossus of Rhodes!

"You don't expect this thing to be permanent, do you?" persisted the man, still fanning himself with his hat.

"Yes, we do," Brother Paul answered, smiling and showing his handsome white teeth. "This colony was planted up here in the wilderness over fifty years ago, with less than a dozen members. Today we have a thousand members; all peaceable and law abiding, many of them unknown are in the outside world aiding in the work of reform, going and coming to this haven of rest, where peace, hope and brotherly love alone prevails."

With the exception of the stout man, the visitors had all gone down and taken the train for the junction, accompanied by Brother Eric and Annie. The stranger stood some moments silently studying the distant landscape, with its thousands of acres of orchards spread out like a grand painting; as his glance swept around taking in the mountain scenery, with the unique, city perched on its elevated site, his eyes kindled, and he said with enthusiasm, "I must go now, but some day I shall come up here alone and stay with you a long time, and study your system."

"You mean our religion," interposed Brother Paul, reaching out and clasping the man's hand in both of his warm magnetic palms; "that is the secret, my brother."

For a moment the two men looked into each other's eyes as they stood thus. God only knows what was revealed to them in that space of time.

The visitor waved his hand, bowed politely to

us all, and without more words turned and walked down to the party that awaited him on the train.

We were silent for some little time, no one apparently caring to break the spell that had fallen upon us.

At length Angela said, "I do not believe that with all their millions those people are as happy as we are, who haven't a dollar in the world that we can call our own."

Brother Paul, who had not lifted his eyes from the ground since the visitor had departed, now said in his impressive manner, "That is the saddest thought in the whole matter; these people are not happy, but are constantly seeking for happiness, driven hither and yon by that spirit of restlessness that always lashes the disobedient soul, driving the individual from one extreme to another."

"What assurance have we that those people come under the head of 'disobedient souls,' as you call them?" I screwed up courage enough to ask.

"Why because they are manifesting the unmistakable signs. They are constantly seeking for some change, they are never satisfied with what they find," the Brother answered kindly.

"The obedient soul has found its heaven within, it is therefore satisfied; it has no further desire to travel over unexplored countries in palace cars, with servants and slaves at beck and call."

"I suppose that what you call 'disobedient souls' are those that go to hell, are they not?" asks a divinity student, looking sharply through his glasses at the Brother.

"No; not as you understand it and teach it," replied the teacher deliberately. "Hell is not a country or a region, but a state. When we cultivate that which makes it, we have it right along, here and now. As we find our heaven within, so on the other hand we find our hell there, whenever we look it up and arrange for it. That creed of an endless hell originated wholly with man, a diabolical type of man too. I do not believe you or I could have framed it. We should have constantly remembered that God, first of all, was Justice; then, first of all, was Love; and love works no ill at any time. One of the foremost laws of God's justice is, that Good is Eternal; that which we term Evil is the outgrowth of the law of transition, so our hell is fleeting, that is what makes hell, I think. When man falls into a line of evil thinking, he begins to go out, he gets in a hurry, he goes with great speed; we hear occasionally of so-and-so being 'fast.' "

"What do you mean by 'going out?' " the young man asked with asperity.

Brother Paul looked at the youth a moment, just as sweetly as an angel, while I could scarcely keep my seat I wanted to go over and box his ears so badly; then the Brother asked in a kindly tone, "What was the matter with your student's lamp in the library last evening when you called me?"

"Why, it went out!" snapped out the young man.

"There must have been a cause for its going out," persisted the teacher.

"Well, you know as well as I do the cause; you know that it had no oil in it."

The boy's face was getting very red, and he was looking a little nonplussed, for as stupid as I was I saw the lesson intended, and evidently it was clear enough to the young Bible student.

"This soul business is the one important matter in man's existence," resumed the teacher. "It is a difficult thing to accept, and still more difficult to try to teach, the fact that at least one-third of the race, as we know it today, has no life beyond this existence any more than the animal creation has. Some of the most beautiful and fascinating people in the world are absolutely without the Ego. They have nothing more lasting in their natures than have their pet horses and dogs. It is all good enough, as far as it goes, but they are the false blossoms on the tree of life, they lack the eternal germ. None were made so; they have grown that way, and they are 'going out,' unless wise love can reclaim them, as in many instances it does."

The great clock sounded the noon hour, and we all started for the Home, and just as we reached the front entrance our people came up from the junction and orchards. Annie and Brother Eric were in advance, and in a high state of glee, getting all the sport they could out of the fact that neither had been invited to remain and dine with the visitors on the palace car.

Nothing ever disturbs Brother Eric, and he had succeeded in infusing his cheer into Annie, so that we all had a jolly time at dinner. I missed John and Brother Rameses from the dining room, and I learned that they had run down to the junction with a pony car loaded with baskets of delicious fruit, cases of honey, bread, butter, cheese, cream and eggs. Annie told me all that.

"That is what I call 'turning the other cheek' with a vengeance," she said, with a malicious twinkle in her eyes. "But as sure as you are born, John will stay down there; their family physician and he went to school together, and I'll wager anything they will make him dine with them."

"Well, I hope they will," I cried, rising up in my pride for John. "I can tell you that none of them are any better than he is, I don't care how many millions they may have."

She began to giggle. "What a fool you are. Did I say that he was not the best man in the world?"

With that she pulled me around, patted my cheeks, hugged and kissed me, wiped away a tear that had come in spite of me, and we mingled our atoms together again and became as one, she promising to tell me all about those "big bugs," what they are like, etc.

THE MUSE OF BROTHERHOOD.

Some momentary touches of my fire
   Have warmed the barren ages with a beam;
There is no peak beyond my swift desire,
   There is no beauty deeper than my dream.

I make an end of life's stupendous jest—
   The merry waste of fortunes by the Few,
While the thin faces of the poor are pressed
   Against the panes—a hungry whirlwind crew.

I come to lift the soul-destroying weight,
   To heal the hurt, to end the foolish loss,
To take the toiler from his brutal fate—
   The toiler hanging on the Labor-Cross.

I bring to earth the feel of home again,
   That men may nestle on her warm, still breast;
I bring to wronged, humiliated men
   The sacred right to labor and to rest.

Still hope for man: my star is on the way!
   Great Hugo saw it from his prison isle;
It lit the mighty dream of Lamennais;
   It shook the ocean thunders of Carlyle.

Wise Greeley touched the star of my desire,
   Great Lincoln knelt before my hidden flame:
It was from me they drew their sacred fire—
   I am Religion by her deeper name.

Edwin Markham.

CHAPTER VIII.

Benares, California, June 24th.

This morning after breakfast I called John to one side and told him I had something of importance that I wished to talk with him about.

He turned me around to the light, and after looking at me sharply for a moment, said, "Well, why not let me hear it right here and now?"

"But somebody will be sure to interrupt us here, and I want you all to myself for a good long talk," said I, with a decided jerk of the head.

John never does anything in a hurry, so he stood some moments looking down, as he kicked the leaves with the toe of his boot. At last he said, "Well, what do you say to our going up and trying one of their Twelve Stations?"

We started up the side of the mountain, where from time to time the brethren had built little arbors, fitting comfortable seats around the sides and training over the trellis an exquisite vine, a native of the mountains, thus making a most desirable spot for quiet and deep study. These beautiful and artistic retreats Annie had christened the "Twelve Stations" from the first. So, after getting above all sound from the Home, we seated ourselves where, it being so early in the morning, we felt sure of being free from interruption.

After we had rested for a time, John said, "Had you anything special that you wished to say to me," sitting back and looking at me keenly.

"Well—yes. It was something about these men up here," I said, fidgetting about on my seat. "Do they ever fall in love with women who come up here?" My face was getting awfully red I knew.

John sat several minutes, not saying a word, but striking his boot with a twig that he had gathered on his way up. At last he said, not looking up, "That depends upon what you understand by the term Love."

"Why, I mean what everybody else does, I suppose," I blurted out, my face getting redder every moment.

"There is so much difference in the way in which people accept that term," he said musingly. "Now, for instance, what sort of a love do you have for me?" squaring himself around and looking me full in the eyes.

"Why!" I exclaimed, starting up, "Why I adore you! But that is not the way that men and women love each other, is it? We wouldn't call that love, would we?" I questioned, in great excitement.

"Well," he asked deliberately, "what would you be willing to sacrifice for me?"

I was pretty well wrought up by this time, but kept my tears back, and as soon as I could control my voice I said, "It is an easy matter for people to talk, John," taking his face between my hands, "but I would die today to save your life and honor." And so I would!

The tears gathered in his honest, kindly eyes, and he said in a gentle, quiet voice, "I do not know of any other love than that, my dear. That excitable, devouring, scathing instinct that usually goes by the name of Love, is of purely animal origin and no more lasting. A large proportion of the marriages of the present day are the spur of that instinct, and hence the unhappiness."

I studied the man earnestly; he had a kind of command about him that appeared to compel one to accept his views, whatever they might be. At length I said, "Do you never intend to marry or to love any one?"

How I do wish I could describe John to you; I never have seen another man so handsome. He has times of looking strange. I do not understand him. He has a smile like no other man.

He caught my hands in his and smiling said, "To marry, no! To love anybody, yes! In the first place, my heart is running over with love for you; then I have a multitude of other friends whom I adore, as you call it. I have so many whom I love that I have no chance to narrow down my affections to one individual."

There must have been a curious expression on my face, for he laughed heartily and said, "What? would you like to have me love and marry some woman who would love and monopolize me, taking me away from you—which she would?"

I did not reply. We sat for some moments in silence, and I recalled Annie and her peculiar disposition to monopolize anyone that she had any claims upon, and I wondered if most wives were not on that same plane.

A sudden fear seized me; I did not want John to marry. Such a thing would be a tragedy to me. But—did I want to marry? No; I do not believe there is a man on earth that I would leave John for, not even Rameses, providing that he was of the marriage sort, which I am pretty sure he is not.

John sat in silence, even forgetting me, I think. How handsome he was, and how proud I was of him! A bell, sounding faintly on the rarified air, recalled us to the outside world again.

"That is the bell for the lesson, and our last one," cried John, springing up. "I want you to take in every word, because it is not every day that we can hear Father Hyacinth."

"I listen to these lessons all for your sake, John," I said, as we entered the chapel and took our seats.

After we were comfortably seated I began to look about for our friends. I saw Annie up in a new seat beside Sir Charles, and the Boston man poked up on a high seat right in the midst of the San Francisco party of girls. Well—in turning around who should be seated just back of us but that blonde beauty, Rameses; I could have touched him with my hand, but I did not. I confessed that I felt happier when I found that he was near by.

If I had thought Father Hyacinth grand in

his previous lessons, I thought him divine in this one. How I wished that all the world could have heard him. What he said that day is indelibly stamped upon my mind; it has become a part of my being.

At the close of the lesson Annie came to me and putting her arms about me, whispered, "Can you forgive me and still love me?" the tears filling her eyes.

I took her to my heart as I recalled our lesson.

> "Long-suffering Lord! Ah, who should be
> Forgiven, if thou wert as we?"
>
> —Pearls of the Faith.

> "If ye forgive men their mistakes, your Father will also forgive you yours. But if ye forgive not men their mistakes, neither will your Father forgive you yours."
>
> —The Gospel of the Lord.

"Christ is coming more and more to be Lord and Master in our social order. * * * * In all the blundering and ignorance of the attempt to create a new social order, I can dimly see Christ re-asserting His Lordship and Mastership in unexpected ways and unexpected places. It is in the New Testament, in the teachings of Christ, that we are to find the Spirit which must pervade and regenerate the social order.

If this be so, if Christ is the heart of the Bible, by whom we are to measure all interpretations and all utterances; * * * * if He is the heart of human history, and human religion; if He is the heart of society, in whose Mastership will be peace and permanent and enduring order; it will be only as He becomes the heart and center and the Life of each one of us, The Good of our being; so that you and I put this Christ before us and say, 'To be like Him,' that is the aim of our life, the inspiration of our being, so that we say with Paul, 'The Love of Christ constraineth us."

—Lyman Abbott.

EIGHTH LESSON.

THE PRODIGAL'S RETURN.

We have now reached the crowning point in this most vital study. To have a perfect knowledge of all the leading facts that have been presented in this series of talks is of little value to the individual if not put into practical use in every-day life. Not alone is the student to make the laws laid down in these lessons his daily precepts, but he must take the one Central Life, illuminating the whole, as his guide in all things. Nay, more, as the one absorbing love of his existence!

Nothing is of real value to the individual unless it be practical. It is very true that the foregoing theories may not be considered practical by the thorough business man of the world, but we do not view matters quite from his standpoint; we have a code of laws which we consider equally as practicable. We take Christ's standard of morals and religion and His daily life as our guide.

A perfect life is not an inheritance or gift; it is not gained by subscribing to creeds, dogmas or ceremonials; and even a conscientious belief in these vital truths will not alone bring the desired state to the individual. There must be a systematic training of the disposition; a reconstruction of the mind, the unfolding of the Divine Mind. This mental training must be just as orderly and as regular as the drilling in our gymnasiums for the purpose of perfecting the physical symmetry and strength of the people of this colony. First of all, the individual must carefully and dispassionately study his own character and line of thought to see where he is deficient and imperfect.

Three years ago, two men came up here in these mountains to be cured of pulmonary disease. They went into our gymnasium, took all of the exercises and full breathing for the purpose of expanding and healing the lungs. In a few months they returned to their homes in perfect health, with the lung tissues healed and the lungs greatly enlarged through their deep breathing of pure air. I speak of those circumstances simply as illustrations of what systematic use will accomplish. The expansion of the lungs, the opening up of air cells that had never been used, changed the whole physical life of those men.

The individual desiring a change of mind—or as it is called in church parlance a "change of heart"—must examine his thoughts and motives to see if he harbors malice, anger, impatience, uncharitableness, greed, egotism, condemnation, love of the world, or a distaste for sacred things. If he finds any of these elements of the carnal mind, he will require good thorough mental gymnastics, and deep thinking to enlarge the mind and heal it of its disease, its sins, its prejudices. He must dwell upon the deeper and spiritual subjects.

He will not like this at first, and will constantly meet with discouragements and rebuffs; just as in the case of these consumptives who came up to take gymnastics; they felt sore and discouraged and irritated at the commencement, but through perseverance at last overcame their enemy, as we have explained. "Whoever will attain to divine contemplation, must mortify the anti-christ in his soul," said Boehme.

It is the bent of the natural man to doubt; he is by physical nature anti-christ. He says, "But I do not believe in Jesus of Nazareth as a Saviour of mankind."

No? You do not believe in Jesus of Nazareth as the Saviour of mankind? And why do you not believe in Him? Have you ever studied His life, character and works? Have you ever thought anything about Him?

We never understand an individual or an object until we have entered into its sphere and viewed it from all quarters. In these days of rapidly evolving ideas and truths, it is scarcely safe for us to doubt or condemn anything simply because we may not see it as presented at the time. In the near future it may be demonstrated as a fact in science, what we have considered but the vagaries of an erratic or half crazed brain.

Once upon a time, centuries ago, a man, a thinker and a dreamer, announced to the world that the earth was a globe, round, instead of flat, and that it turned upon its axis and traveled around its center the sun. And the whole reading world rose up against him and cried out, "We do not believe it! It is not true! You shall take it back!" and he took it back to save his life. But today no one has the courage to deny or doubt that statement concerning the earth's form or orbit. The vagaries of today become the scientific facts of tomorrow. It does not make a fact any the less a fact simply because we do not happen to believe it.

I appreciate the truth that many are attracted to this line of teaching through a Theosophical bias, yet will not at once be interested in the history and the mission of the Christ. And to scores of so-called Christians also His life, mission, death and resurrection, have been presented in a manner so obscure and unnatural as to have made no permanent impression upon their minds, so that they are really unacquainted with His character and teachings, and are literally without Him. He is, to all such, unfamiliar, inaccessible and of no vital interest.

The Mosaic law suits the average human mind best, and Christ's simple, straightforward and just doctrines have not been the burden of the teaching of the modern religious world. We hear from the pulpits of the land all about Moses, Elias, Job, Jeremiah, Zechariah, and hosts of others; some of whom were great prophets and seers, and some, alas! shedders of human blood, who lived away back in the dead past; but we are told very little about the Christ who was in reality the consummation of all that past history, and who came to do away with the conditions then existing. Christ in His fullness has never been preached to the world. We have not been made acquainted with Him. His helpful human side has rarely been depicted by religious teachers. The human family is longing for a more intimate knowledge of the human Jesus, without knowing the cause of its dissatisfaction and uneasiness. It is as a child lost in a desert place sighing and sobbing for the devoted and loving parent.

We, being men and human, are dull of comprehension of spiritual things, can only come to the Christ through the man Jesus: we must come into an intimate knowledge of His human nature; of His deep love toward all, His pity for the sorrowing, His keen sense of justice, His tenderness to the babes and little children, His sympathy for the common folk, for the unfortunate, sinful and outcasts; His modesty and humility, but above all His boundless love.

There have been many noble and devoted teachers of men, in all ages, but there has never been one who presented such an example of unselfish devotion, such a high sense of justice, such wisdom, such love for and understanding of man's needs, as did Jesus the Christ.

Beyond all reasons that the human mind can urge, there is that deep-down secret cause why

He understood man's nature and needs better than anyone else ever did or could; because the race in its divine nature is His, is joined to Him and He to it, as loving children are bound to the adoring and devoted parent. And man, in his spiritual nature, is constantly longing for that Infinite Source, without knowing—in the condition he now is—what it is he is yearning for; while Christ is longing—beyond anything that we can comprehend—for the love and recognition of His children.

The teachings of our Lord in the Gospel of John has never been clear under any other interpretation. How impressive it all becomes when we understand why Christ, of all others, came to redeem the race and restore all things. He is saying to you all at this moment: "Come unto me, and be taught of me; and your lives shall find a resting place. My yoke is easy, and my burden light." Come unto Me, He pleads.

Now come with me for a little season, and let us live over again with Jesus that Judean life. Let us walk with Him beside the blue Galilean waters, under the sunny skies. Let us accept Him for our Teacher, Master and Leader. Let us get very near to Him; He permits it. John leaned upon His breast and was not forbidden.

And you, frail little one, you may slip your cold, weak hand into His warm, strong one and feel yourself gently led and comforted without words. And you sick, suffering and sinful ones may touch the hem of His robe and find yourselves healed. And I—I will ask only the privilege of tying the straps of His sandals, and shall be blessed, strengthened and comforted thereby.

We will become His disciples, for He refused none. So day after day by the seashore, on the hillside, through the fields of grain, on the mountain-top, in the Temple, in the busy marts of trade, we will follow His footsteps and listen to His teachings of love, mercy, wisdom and the brotherhood of man.

We will behold how multitudes of the afflicted, deformed and sinful follow Him, and hang upon His words, imbibing them as drops of healing and eternal life. We will see Him feed the multitude, refusing none and blessing all. And we will gaze into His tender eyes until our own fill and overflow with tears, shed in sympathy for the struggling, human mass that do not know Him.

Then we will seat ourselves upon the grass with the multitude that hang upon His words, and, oh! the music of that voice! Who could resist it?

"Come unto me all you laboring and burdened ones * * * and be taught of me, for my yoke is easy and my burden is light. * * * If any one love me, he will observe my words; and the Father will love him, and we will come unto him and make our abode with him."

We listen eagerly, the tears rolling down our faces and washing out of our hearts the uncharitable feelings and all unkindness toward our brothers. As He stands before us, we note how majestic He appears; and yet how tender and gentle toward the frail and suffering ones. How carressingly He holds the tiny infant in His strong arms. How they trust and love Him. How grand! How more than human He appears; and yet how near He seems to us all.

How our hearts are stirred as He says, "A new commandment give I unto you, That you love one another, as I have loved you. By this shall all men know that you are my disciples, if you have love one to another. I will ask the Father, and He will give you another helper that He may be with you forever; the Spirit of Truth, which the world cannot receive because it beholds it not, nor knows it; but you know it, because it abides with you and will be in you * * and bring all things to your remembrance whatsoever I have said unto you."

Then He feeds the multitude and sends them to their homes refreshed, blessed and healed.

So we, who hang upon His words, follow Him day by day, and our souls are thrilled with new and more humane thoughts, and life appears so different to us; we see how selfish and thoughtless we have been, and we long to live better and truer lives. So we follow our Guide along through the groves of olive and citron, and up the sunny hillside, and we all seat ourselves about the beloved Master; and He reveals to us, His chosen ones, the deep secrets of His mission to the children of men, and His real relation to them. We feel ourselves being healed as He says to us in His tender tones, "In my Father's house there are many dwellings; but if not, I would have told you; because I am going to prepare a place for you. * * * So that where I am you also may be. All that the Father giveth me shall come to me. I come down from heaven, not to do mine own will, but the will of Him who sent me. Greater love hath no other than this, that one should lay down his life in behalf of his friends. You did not choose me, but I chose you, and appointed you, that you may go and bear fruit, and that your fruit may abide."

We cannot leave Him; His love draws us with an irresistible power. We watch Him at the well in His interview with the Samaritan woman, and we tremble as He reads her soul record; and we try to cast off our selfhood, knowing that He sees all our thoughts. Then we remember Mary Magdalene and how He looked at her without uttering a word, and how she was stripped of her scarlet robes and sinful ways—healed without a touch. And we remember the centurion's servant, and we long to even touch the hem of His garments and be healed of our infirmities.

As we follow Him over the hillsides and through the fields, listening to His teaching, we gradually come into the full consciousness that Love is the redeeming breath of heaven. He turns and faces us; as we eagerly cluster about Him His countenance is radiant, His voice sweet and gentle, as He says, "This is my commandment, that you love each other, as I loved you. No man has greater love than this, That one should lay down his life in behalf of his friends."

And now, as we return to the present, do we not all feel refreshed and strengthened? Do we not feel that we know Christ the better for having dwelt with Him a little season? We feel that we have touched the hem of His garments, have felt His touch upon our heads; we have gazed into His eyes, and He has smiled upon us. He has said, "You my beloved have not chosen me, but I have chosen you."

All your life long you will carry the memory of this brief visit with our divine Master. There will be aroused in the breast of each a tender pity if not a love for Him. We will be unable to understand how one so good, kind, patient and harmless could have been so misunderstood and wronged. In time, as we go into our seasons of meditations and give ourselves up to these thoughts, we will become conscious of an exalted Presence near us, filling us with new emotions such as we have never experienced before.

In our study of Jesus, the Man, we have come into consciousness of the divine Christ, and there will creep into our hearts a feeling to which we have been strangers; we shall be slowly approaching our transformation, our "new birth;" we will begin to feel a greater patience for the faults and weaknesses of others, a tenderness and pity for all that has life and consciousness. A pity that will not permit us to tread upon a worm.

This will be the dawning of love so broad that it will embrace all humanity; will recognize all men and women as brothers and sisters, regardless of condition, position, race or color. A love that will cause us to sacrifice the self for the good of another; that judges no man, but will help us to bear and forbear in silence and patience. We shall no longer have the ambition to accumulate earthly possessions; but, instead, will experience a strong desire to help lighten the burden of the oppressed wherever found, recognizing in all the common bond of brotherhood, seeing in the lowly and degraded only the children of an infinitely loving Father. We feel ourselves fired with a new zeal for good works, and deep down in secret we feel a nameless adoration for our newly found Friend, The Christ. He has taken up His abode with us. Long and silently He has waited for us to recognize Him, and open unto Him. He has said, "Behold, I stand at the door and knock; if any man hear my voice and open the door, I will come in to him and sup with him and he with me."

We cannot fail to grow like unto that which we constantly contemplate and love.

"What thou lovest, O man!
That too become thou must.
God, if thou lovest God;
Dust, if thou lovest dust."

We become possessed with the desire to imitate the deeds of those whom we respect and love. An absorbing love for Christ and humanity is an evidence that there has taken place in the soul a healing process through the inflowing of the Christ life. This is that regeneration or "new birth" of which we have spoken. This is not an impossible condition, this at-onement with Christ; there are hosts of noble examples where both men and women have entered into this state of consciousness of the nearness of Christ, and the infusion of His strength and life into their's in time of sore trial. Such have been among the philosophers, philanthropists, teachers and helpers of the race, beside a multitude of unnamed and unknown mystics in the obscure walks of life. It is a subdued and elevated state of mind, wherein exists the deepest satisfaction, a nameless serenity, which no amount of misunderstanding and persecution from the world, losses by land or sea, disloyalty or desertion on the part of friends, can in the least disturb. Unto such is given to know the secrets of the "kingdom of God." "And you shall find rest unto your souls."

Sponoza, while hiding from his religious persecutors, living in poverty and isolation, subsisting on a crust of bread and a cup of milk or water as his daily rations, said, with the zeal of an enthusiast: "I never dreamed it possible for a human being to be so happy as I am." In his expanded and awakened soul he beheld the truth of Divine Being. His soul was exalted by a deep and fervent love for the Divine; he had come into consciousness of the new life of his Christ-likeness.

It is a historical fact that the most enlightened, advanced and highly developed minds in all Christendom have and do believe in Christ; in His divine nature, His perfection, and the majority of them in His office as Saviour of mankind.

But this changed condition should not take you from among your brethren. You are to radiate this new power within you, as did Christ while He was Jesus the man, and walked among men. He has given you an example: He says to you: "You are my friends, if you do whatsoever things I command you. I have chosen you, and ordained you, that you should go and bring forth fruit."

This is a deeply significant epoch in the experience of the race. Much questioning, uneasiness and speculation is the impulse of the hour, and infidelity is the curse of modern thought. Man requires a central object of contemplation because the law of centralization governs the substance of his being.

Christ was the manifestor of all life in our center, and is as much individual as the great central sun of our universe, and as real as you or I; and more than that, walks with men upon the earth today as He did two thousand years ago.

Men have been looking for and expecting the return of Christ for, lo! these many generations, and have not understood that to the pure in heart He is always near and ready to bless. He is saying to us all, I will not leave you orphans; I am coming to you. "Yet a little while, and the world beholds me no more: but you behold me; because I live, you also shall live."

"If any one loves me, he will observe my word, and my Father will love him, and we will come to him and make our abode with him." Could there be anything clearer to the comprehension than this promise? These promises are for every hour and for every individual soul on earth. They were not for a few fishermen two thousand years ago; but for all who are seeking for the truth.

Christ is love, and love is for the healing of the nation. All who are without faith and a love for Christ, are as a ship in mid-ocean; storm-tossed, without rudder or compass, at the mercy of the gale. There is in all such a nameless longing for they know not what.

Such may possess riches, honor, knowledge, wisdom, and yet be without peace. Peace never comes to the soul of man until he has opened his inner consciousness to Christ; because we are His, and His likeness is stamped upon our inmost soul. He is constantly pleading for the return of His children, to be recognized and loved. He does not command, He pleads.

"Behold I have stood at the door, and I knock; if anyone may have heard my voice, and opened the door, I will enter in to him, and feast with him, and he with me."

"The love of the perfect man is a universal love; a love whose scope is all mankind."

—Confucius.

"Blessed are the Peacemakers; for they shall be called the children of God.

Love * * * bless * * * do good, that ye may be the children of your Father, who is in heaven."

—Jesus.

"Then shall all the tribes of the earth mourn, and they shall see the Son of man coming in the clouds of heaven, with power and great glory. And he shall send forth his messengers with a great sound of a trumpet, and they shall gather together his elect from the four winds, from one end of heaven to the other."

— Matthew xxiv. 30, 31.

Benares, California, June 30th.

Today, on the eleven o'clock train, a party of tourists came to attend the opening of the Observatory. It was composed of scientific men and their wives, not alone from Los Angeles, but from several other large cities. The ladies were cultured and accomplished, the gentlemen all solid scientific men. Our German professor found himself in his element, and the Boston man never so much as looked at me, or one of the common individuals. Father Hyacinth, Brother Rameses and Brother Paul are to take charge of the party, and preparations have been made for them to remain all night at the Observatory. As there is an evidence of a cloudless night, it will be a wondrous treat to all. We are promised the same a few nights later.

After dinner, as the party was taking its departure for the Observatory, we noticed that among the number were the Westlakes, the German professor, the Boston man and the San Francisco party. They were all in exuberant spirits and presented a picture which I shall never forget as they all set out up the mountain, each woman carrying her basket of refreshments, and each man with a sufficient supply of bedding strapped across his shoulders.

After they had passed out of sight, John gathered our party, Angela, Annie and myself, about him, with an air full of foreboding of some kind of change. I have a deadly terror of changes. He gathered us about him as close as he could, and managed to get hold of a hand of each, and then began to unfold his business.

"You see," he began, "I received a letter to-day from August, and he says, 'That I had better come home, the harvest is unusually large, and he doesn't know how to manage it.' We have overstayed the time allotted to us already, and as the lessons are closed for this session, I think we had better go down to our little plantation and see what August and Elsie are doing. What do you say, girls?"

No one uttered a word. He looked from one to another in blank amazement.

After studying our downcast faces for a moment or two he broke into a hearty laugh, exclaiming, "Well upon my word! Do you want to stay here?" still shaking with laughter.

"We like to stay here," said Annie sheepishly; "but we cannot stay without you."

We all laughed heartily at this change in Annie's sentiments regarding the colony.

"How is it with you, girls?" asked John, turning to Angela and myself.

"So far as I am concerned," I exclaimed impulsively, "where you go I shall go, and where you stay I shall stay."

Angela remained silent a time, as was her habit; she was always deliberate in her conclusions.

We were all silent for some moments, when John said, "You girls might remain here, and I go East and attend to matters and return here in December. I am to remain with them up here for another year. It is my desire to join the brotherhood if my girls are not opposed," smiling upon us.

"I have from the first decided to remain permanently in the School," said Angela. "It is what I have long been in search of."

"And you know that what is for you, is for me," I said to John, snuggling up close to him.

I wish I could portray in words John's face when a certain smile of satisfaction lights it up; it is a species of inward illumination; it always recalls that story of Christ and His three on the mountains, "And His face did shine as the sun."

I have seen but few faces that would express so much, and John's is among the number.

After a little silence he asked Annie what arrangements would please her, and after due deliberation she concluded to remain in the fraternity until John and I should return; and feeling it to be good for her to be in the atmosphere of this body of people, we considered it as satisfactorily settled.

Benares, California, July 1st.

The sun had just risen when the scientific party reached the Home where breakfast awaited them.

It appears that a large portion of the visitors had decided to examine the mountain lake which supplied water for irrigation and all purposes on the plantation. Brother Frederick and John were to act as escorts on this occasion. The Westlakes, the San Francisco party, and as many of the excursionists as were sufficiently rested, together with most of our late class, started up the mountain in an entirely new direction. We followed a roadway for a mile or more through wild and sublime scenery; at length we came to what appeared to have been the crater of an extinct volcano; a deep oval basin with stone walls of almost uniform depth, and so smooth as to appear like the work of human hands. These almost perpendicular walls enclosed an area of about thirty acres, forming a uniform body of the clearest and purest of water; no vegetation growing near the water, but a fringe of evergreen at the top of the wall. There were various speculations among the scientists as to its source of supply. Some believe it to be a reservoir for the melted snows, others consider that it is supplied entirely from springs. Father Hyacinth, who has watched it carefully for the past thirty years, says that it has never perceptibly fluctuated in that time, and that in the center they are unable to sound it. The water is almost as cold as ice while in the lake, but becomes sufficiently warmed for irrigating purposes before reaching the plantation.

I have no words with which to express my sensations while standing on the outer rim of that strange body of water. It was grand beyond expression; in fact, too grand for me; it gave me a sense of some unexplainable mystery, awesome in the extreme.

What had formed this strange reservoir? Had this once been the South Pole? Who could tell? I felt dumb in the presence of this mystery. Many of the party were full of speculations and suggestions, and some of them stopped talking long enough only to take breath. If they were impressed with the sublimity of the scene, it did not silence them.

I expanded my lungs and breathed with delight when I reached the Home, and saw the familiar signs of life and the work of human hands, and recalled Annie's remark when John asked her to join the party:

"No, I thank you; I do not wish to go to any higher region just now; I consider this the jumping off place." But thereby hangs a tale.

I had discovered that Sir Charles had dropped out of the party and lingered behind, which accounted for Annie's lack of interest in the upper region.

After one of our superb dinners—which was in reality a banquet, so lavishly and exquisitely was it served—the party took their leave, full of enthusiasm and admiration for everything and everybody; and we all equally enthused and in love with them.

Such experiences cannot fail to bring out the

strongest and best that there is in human nature. The grand in nature always develops the grand in man. I had never realized before that there were so many people that were given to large thoughts. I had fancied that John and Angela were two cranks who had ideas unlike anybody else in the world, and fancied that in the end it might land them both in the insane asylum. But here were hundreds of people, all perfectly at home and all happy, entertaining those advanced and ultra ideas and plans, and all appeared perfectly sane.

I had lived in a superficial world, such as the larger portion of the human family exist in, I think, where to eat and drink and clothe oneself is, as a rule, the end and aim of life; but a few months' experience here has opened up to me a vast world of ideas, which under the old circumstances would have been an unexplored and unknown region of thought and life.

Those who have ascended the mountain of life can never again descend and be at peace on the low lands and marshes. To climb is the instinct of man. Ever more give us light! is the prayer.

Benares, California, July 16th.

Tomorrow, John and myself take our departure for our eastern home, returning here in September instead of December, as at first arranged.

Annie has no desire to return East at present, so she informed me this morning, saying that she considered her fate was sealed. In what way it was done she did not inform me, so I asked her if it was hermetically sealed. She elevated her nose and walked away with an air of injured innocence, not deigning to reply. She has had a great number of similar attacks, so that I am not at all alarmed. She told John last night that she considered herself as good as engaged to Sir Charles, and John having her under his care in a degree talked around the young nobleman to see what he thought about the matter, and finds him entirely unconscious of the young lady's state of mind, and so far has no intention of changing his present free state.

Angela tells me that Annie is hard at work on a manuscript which she intends having published at once. She intends writing up her experience with this community. We can imagine what it will be like. It will be after the order of "Innocents Abroad," I conclude, as she sees only the ludicrous side of life. But Annie has grown more earnest and truthful, and I feel sure that she will come out all right.

Yesterday afternoon I had a long and earnest conversation with Father Hyacinth. He told me all about the new colony that has been established in the West. A new plant, he calls it. Ten thousand acres of land have been appropriated, and the city laid out and planned by their architect. Brother Rameses, Brother Paul and John have been chosen to get the colony in working order. Father Hyacinth starts for the new territory at once, and a supply of assistants will go there as soon as required.

This new arrangement does not give me the slightest trouble, for I have made up my mind to go where John does. Then, too, Rameses is going, and I cannot help but feel an interest in that fellow—nobody could that ever saw him.

It is my intention to return with John to this community and perhaps take up the history of this wonderful people; especially the working of the new colony, for I feel sure that they are in the right and that through their teachings and practices the world will be made better, and in time, so potent is the influence of Mind, the race must be redeemed.

DESCRIPTION OF JESUS CHRIST BY PUBLIUS LENTULUS, PRESIDENT OF JUDEA IN THE REIGN OF TIBERIUS CAESAR.

There lives at this time, in Judea, a man of singular virtue, whose name is Jesus Christ, whom the barbarians esteem as a prophet, but his followers love and adore him as the offspring of the immortal God. He calls back the dead from their graves, and heals all sorts of diseases with a word or a touch. He is a tall man, and well-shaped, of an amiable and reverend aspect; his hair of a color that can hardly be matched, falling into graceful curls, waving about, and very agreeably couching upon his square shoulders, parted on the crown of his head, running as a stream to the front, after the fashion of the Nazarites; his forehead high, large and rather imposing; his cheeks without spot or wrinkle, beautiful with a lovely red; his nose and mouth formed with exquisite symmetry; his beard thick and of a color suitable to his hair, reaching below his chin and parting in the middle like a fork; his eyes bright and blue, clear and serene; look, innocent, dignified, manly and mature; in proportion of body most perfect and captivating; his hands and arms most delicate to behold. He rebukes with majesty, counsels with mildness; his whole address, whether in word or deed, being eloquent and grave. No man has seen him laugh, yet his manners are exceedingly pleasant; but he has wept frequently in the presence of men. He is temperate, modest and wise; a man, for his extraordinary beauty and divine perfections, surpassing the children of men in every sense.

Lightning Source UK Ltd.
Milton Keynes UK
UKHW020036301118
333214UK00014B/1542/P